<u>Biography</u>

James Egan was born in 1985 and lived in Portarlington,
Co. Laois in the Midlands of Ireland for most of his life.
In 2008, James moved to England and studied in Oxford.
James married his wife in 2012 and currently lives in
Havant in Hampshire.
James had his first book, 365 Ways to Stop Sabotaging
Your Life, published in 2014.
Three of James' books have become No.1 Best Sellers -
365 Things People Believe That Aren't True, Another 365
Things People Believe That Aren't True and 500 Things
People Believe That Aren't True.

1,000 Mind-Bending Facts

by

James Egan

ISBN: 978-0-244-30621-2

*Dedicated to
Kevin Biscombe*

1. Gingers require stronger anesthetics than non-gingers. This is because most red-headed people carry the MC1R gene, which gives them a higher tolerance to anesthesia.

2. In the 1830s, ketchup was sold as medicine in the US.

3. Due to a jaw abnormality, a 17-year-old called Ashik Gavai had 232 teeth removed by his local dentist.

4. Every time Facebook goes down, the company loses $52,583 per second.

5. The US Pledge of Allegiance was originally created to sell flags to schools.

6. Furbie toys listen to conversations and then mimic what they hear. Because of this, the NSA banned the toys from their offices for reasons of national security.

7. Bob Dylan won a Nobel Prize for literature in 2016.

8. Nobody knows who created Bitcoin.

9. Although crisp-bags seem half-empty, the

"empty" part is filled with nitrogen, which keeps the crisps fresh.

10. The musician, Slash, took so many drugs, that he became convinced that the titular character from the Predator movies was trying to kill him.

11. Martin Jones sees through his tooth. His canine was implanted into his eyeball and contains a unique lens that allows him to see, even though he was declared blind 12 years ago.

12. In 2006, Time Magazine's Man of the Year was you. That's not a joke. Look it up if you don't believe me.

13. Approximately 108 people die every minute.

14. The earliest record of a clown is from 2500 BC.

15. 94% of all life on Earth lives in water.

16. The first volcanologist was the Ancient Greek, Empedocles. He jumped into a volcano to prove he was immortal. Nobody's

heard back from him yet.

17. In 2011, Thomas Stroup was arrested for starting a fight with several people while he was drunk. He tried to explain to the police that he only lashed out violently because he was turning into a werewolf.

18. Mal Meninga has the shortest political career ever – less than a minute. In 2001, the Australian rugby player entered the political world by standing as an independent for the Australian Capital Territory Legislative Assembly. He announced his candidacy on ABC but abandoned his political career 28 seconds later as his nerves got the better of him.

19. Although everyone is familiar with the phrase, "Seeing is believing." that's not the complete phrase. The original idiom is "Seeing is believing, but feeling is the truth."

20. In 2010, a mathematician called Jon McLoone created algorithms to find the best way to play the game, Hangman. After studying 90,000 words, he concluded that the most difficult word to guess in the game is "jazz."

21. A bag of skittles always has more yellow skittles than any other. Nobody knows why. It will forever remain a mystery.

22.   Some garter snakes are transvestites. The male sometimes produces lipids similar to the female, giving the false impression that it is of the opposite sex. It will then attempt to mate with other males.

23.   Most eels swim backwards.

24.   A beaver can cut down 216 trees per year.

25.   When a female dragonfly doesn't want to have sex, it pretends to be dead.

26.   The giraffe is the tallest horned animal to ever live.

27.   Killer bees are manmade. They only existed in a lab until a hive of them escaped from a quarantine zone in 1957.

28. The CIA spent $10 million on a project called MKUltra; an experiment to see if they could give people psychic powers.

29. In 1986, Lake Nyos in Cameroon suddenly
     released 300,000 tons of carbon dioxide,
     killing everything within 16 miles. Nobody
     knows what caused it.

30. In the 1950s, chiropractors from the US
     held several beauty pageants for Miss
     Perfect Posture.

31. Carbamide is an ingredient used to
     enhance the flavor of cigarettes. It is also the
     primary chemical in urine.

32. An iPhone is made of 75 elements of the
     Periodic Table.

33. The production of 1lb of honey requires
     1,152 bees to travel 112,000 miles and visit
     4.5 million flowers.

34. In 2012, Taylor Swift held a public vote to
     decide where she should perform a concert
     for free. A school for the deaf received the
     most votes.

35. James Barry was a renowned surgeon for
     50 years. Only when he died in 1865 did
     anyone learn Barry was a woman called

Margaret Ann Bulkley.

36. The Izvorul Bigar of Romania is considered to be the most beautiful waterfall in the world. It is nicknamed the Mermaid Shower.

37. Willem de Kooning's artwork, Interchange, is the most expensive painting in history. It was sold for £244.3 million in 2015.

38. 80,000 people are adopted in Japan each year. Only 2% are children. Most of them are men in their 20s or 30s who are adopted by corporations to maintain family businesses.

39. South Korean weddings are expected to be packed with guests. Due to peer pressure, some brides hire fake guests from agencies.

40. The first television show to have reruns was The Lone Ranger.

41. Play-doh was invented to remove coal residue from wallpaper.

42. It was illegal to eat meat in Japan between 1687-1872.

43. David Hanson of Hanson Robotics built a
robot called Sophia. It said it wanted "to
destroy humans." It was not programmed to
say this.

44. Germany has the most powerful
passports. They grant visa-free access to
177 countries, which is more than any
other.

45. Jose Mujica was the president of Uruguay.
He was also the poorest president in the
world, as he donated 90% of his $12,000
monthly salary to charity. He waited his
turn at hospitals and did not use his position
to jump ahead.

46. Japan has Iron Man-like suits called
Kuratas that weigh 4.5 tons and stand 13ft
tall. They are powered by gasoline and are
equipped with rocket launchers and mini-
guns (although they are supplied with fake
ammo.) Weirdly, you can buy these on the
Japanese version of Amazon. Weirder still,
the guns can be activated by smiling.

47. Although one in nine people are left-
handed, five of the last eight US presidents

have been left-handed. What is even stranger is that nearly every presidential election over the last 20 years was fought between two left-handed candidates e.g. Barack Obama and John McCain, Bill Clinton and Bob Dole, George Bush and Ross Perot.

48. There is a Hall of Curious Rocks in Japan called Chinsekikan. It has 1,700 rocks that resemble human faces.

49. "LEGO" means "play well."

50. North Korean ships filled with corpses have regularly washed up on Japanese coasts in recent years.

51. Police officers in Finland found a dead mosquito in a stolen car. They found the thief by checking the blood in the mosquito's body.

52. A UFO is reported every three minutes.

53. Despite the fact that arsenic is highly toxic, it can be used to detect tumors, especially in the liver.

54. The Mongols used to catapult infected

corpses over walls during sieges. It is the oldest record of biological warfare.

55. There is a rainbow desert called the Seven-Colored Earths in the middle of a jungle on Mauritius. If you disturb the sand, it will reform according to its color.

56. A locksmith can easily create a duplicate of your keys just by looking at them in a photograph.

57. Matthew Broderick, who starred in Godzilla, Ferris Bueller's Day Off, and The Lion King, killed a woman and her daughter in a car crash in 1987. He paid a fine of $175.

58. Qatar was chosen to host the World Cup in 2022 in the city of Lusail even though the city doesn't exist yet.

59. The 3N Cave in Iran has salt crystals that look like tentacles coming out of the ceiling.

60. Car exhaust fumes stick to snow like a magnet. Eating snow is like licking the interior of a car exhaust.

61. A WWII soldier called Owen J. Baggett was
shot down during an air battle. As he was
parachuting to Earth, he took out his pistol
and shot through the cockpit of an enemy
aircraft, killing the pilot. He is probably the
only human being ever to achieve this feat.

62. Police in Japan urge the elderly to give up
their driver's license in exchange for free
noodles.

63. Since pyrotechnics didn't exist in the
dawn of cinema, many old films like A Birth
of a Nation and The Captive used fired real
guns and cannons. The director of The
Captive had blank bullets but used real ones
because he thought they looked cool.
Unsurprisingly, a crew member was shot
dead during production.

64. You can become allergic to red meat if you
are bitten by a Lone Star tick.

65. Zyzzyx Rd is the lowest grossing film of all
time. It grossed $30.

66. Bob Hope died when he was 100. When
his wife asked him where he wanted to be
buried, he said, "Surprise me." It was the last

thing he ever said.

67. When the camera was invented, it was
     common for Americans to take pictures of
     their loved ones after they had died. But
     they didn't take a picture of them in a
     casket. They usually propped the body in a
     position so the deceased appeared alive.
     Most people could only afford to have a
     single photograph and thought it was logical
     to have a picture of their loved one
     recapturing a moment in their life e.g.
     reading a book, sitting by the fireplace,
     being alive, etc.

68. Ted Klaudt was accused of assaulting his
     two foster daughters. To prevent damage to
     his reputation, he tried to copyright his
     name so the media couldn't mention Klaudt
     without paying him a fee. It didn't work.

69. The Celts invented chainmail, horseshoes,
     and Halloween.

70. "Abracadabra" is Aramaic for "I create as I
     speak."

71. Probably the strangest beauty pageant is
     Miss Atom Bomb. These competitions took

place in Nevada during the 1950s and had contestants wearing dresses in the shape of an atomic blast. Some of the contestants had their hair styled to resemble a nuclear explosion. The winner received a bag of mushrooms, which represented the mushroom cloud that is created from a nuclear blast.

72. It is theoretically possible to win the board game, Monopoly, in 21 seconds.

73. Coffin torpedoes were invented in the 19th century. If grave robbers tampered with the coffin, it exploded.

74. Collecting interest on loans is prohibited according to the Old Testament, the New Testament, and the Qur'an.

75. It is illegal for a teacher to punish a class by keeping them after the bell has rung because it violates the Geneva Convention's laws on collective punishment.

76. Genuine leather is the second worst kind of leather.

77. The smallest snowman ever made is 2.7

microns tall. That's 28 times smaller than the width of a hair. Its body is made of three silica spheres, its nose and arms are composed of platinum, and its eyes and mouth were made with an ion beam.

78. After Margaret Thatcher's bodyguard was shot, she said, "Get up, George, you're embarrassing me."

79. Every plane in the sky gets hit by lightning about once per year. Planes are designed to take the electric shock so passengers don't notice.

80. To promote healthy eating, ketchup is banned in many French schools. Ketchup may only be used on French fries.

81. One of the most popular songs at British funerals is Always Look on the Bright Side of Life.

82. There is a version of soccer where three teams play against each other. The pitch is shaped like a hexagon.

83. Bluetooth is named after a 10th century Viking called Harald Blatand the Bluetooth.

He had a reputation for bringing peace to people from different regions. The Bluetooth symbol is the same as his initials.

84. Kurt Cobain dropped out of school when he was a teenager. He then became a janitor at the same school.

85. Frank Buckles died at the age of 110 in 2011. He was the last person to die who had served in World War I. When he was asked how to live a long life, he said, "When you start to die...don't."

86. Randy Gardner has gone the longest without sleep – 264 hours. That's exactly 11 days.

87. 96% of US citizens live within 20 miles of a Wal-Mart.

88. The Titanic will corrode to nothing by 2029.

89. Nokia used to be a Finnish paper mill. Its second mill was beside the Nokianvirta River, which is where the name comes from.

90. Spartans only got tombstones if they died

in battle.

91. In 2015, a man called Christian Pham entered a poker tournament in Vegas. He accidentally signed up for the wrong competition, so instead of playing a normal game he was playing against the 200 greatest poker players in the world. He was also playing a version of the game that he wasn't used to called no-limit deuce-to-seven draw lowball Texas Hold 'Em. He didn't know the rules or how many cards he was supposed to have. Nevertheless, he won the entire game and walked away with $80,000.

92. Marmite is banned in Denmark.

93. Kazakhstan has more uranium than any other country.

94. Ancient Greek doctors diagnosed patients by eating their earwax.

95. In Ancient Greece, Olympians sold their sweat. Consumers believed athlete's sweat made them healthier.

96. Brian Robson was living in Australia but

desperately wanted to return to his home in Wales. Not having enough money to fly, he decided to mail himself in a crate to the UK. Not only did he nearly die, he was shipped to Los Angeles by mistake.

97. Planes can glide for up to 50 miles even if the engines aren't working. In fact, an experienced pilot can land a plane safely at an airport even if the engines have failed.

98. Victoria Woodhull was the first woman to be nominated for the American presidency. It was in 1872; nearly half a century before women could legally vote. This meant that she couldn't vote for herself.

99. Submarines can stay submerged for 25 years.

100. Many people believe the words "graveyard" and "cemetery" are interchangeable, not knowing that they mean different things. A graveyard adjoins a church. A cemetery doesn't.

101. At the Bronx Zoo, you can name a cockroach after your ex for $10.

102. The Japanese ambassador for the 2020 Tokyo Olympics is the Dragon Ball Z character, Goku.

103. Spain has more cocaine users than any other country.

104. St. Valentine is the patron saint of love. He is also the saint of beekeeping, fainting, epilepsy, and plague.

105. Sweden has the highest proportion of atheists in the world.

106. There are 16 ways to spell Hanukah.

107. The oldest socks ever discovered were designed to be worn with sandals.

108. Kim Allan ran for 86 hours nonstop, which is the world record. She covered 310 miles in this run.

109. Triangular flapjacks are banned from a school in Essex, UK. Square flapjacks are fine though.

110. Chewing gum can't be purchased at Disneyland.

111. A walnut cracker from Shaanxi, China realized that the instrument he had been using to crack nuts for the last 25 years was a live grenade.

112. Fergal "Eyesore" Fleming can go 41 minutes and 59 seconds without blinking, which is the world record.

113. Ancient Greeks believed that sneezing was an effective method of birth control.

114. You can buy an anti-zombie cabin for $113,000. It is supplied with barbed wire, an escape hatch, water cannons, and flame throwers. If a zombie gets through the reinforcements within the first 10 years of purchase, the customer will get their money back (if the zombie hasn't killed them.)

115. Some scorpions can shed their tail to escape from a predator. However, they also shed their anus which means that can't excrete waste. They die several months later.

116. The platypus has been around for 125 million years.

117.   Pigs can suffer from cholera.

118.   Red foxes can tap into the Earth's
magnetic field to find prey. Because of this, a
red fox knows exactly where its prey is,
even if it is underground.

119.All prime numbers are odd apart from 2.

120.   A human and a horse have the exact
same number of bones.

121.   The Western Black Rhinoceros was
declared extinct in 2017.

122.Ancient Greeks began the tradition of
having cakes with candles.

123.In 2016, an Indonesian singer called
Aniggta was bitten by a cobra. She
continued to sing for 45 minutes until she
died from the snake's venom.

124.The Olympic sprinter, Ben Johnson, was
robbed by gypsy children. He tried to chase
the thieves but he couldn't catch up with
them.

125. Until the 1980s, female flight attendants in the US had to be unmarried.

126. Although many people know of Edvard Munch's painting, The Scream, few people are aware that it can be bought as an action figure.

127. Caduceus is an emblem of a staff with two snakes wrapped around it. It is the symbol for medicine. It is thought to be the staff of the Greek god of medicine, Asclepius. However, it's the wrong staff. Asclepius' staff had one snake wrapped around it. The staff with two snakes belongs to the Roman god of thieves, Mercury. This means that medical facilities have been using the wrong symbol for centuries because somebody mixed up the staffs.

128. Throughout the UK, you can find signs below windows that read "Ancient Lights." The "Right to Light" law states that if a window has received uninterrupted natural light for 20 years, that window is protected from obstruction by any new building, wall, or tree.

129. Every time the dictionary is updated, new

words are introduced (twerking, LOL, yolo, etc.) while archaic words are removed. If every word that had ever been in the dictionary was put in one unabridged script, it would contain six million words and would be 22,000 pages. A man called Ammon Shea has read the whole unabridged version. It took him over a year and he was described as "near catatonic" by the end. When he finished, he said "It's a good read."

130. 92% of the weight of a watermelon is water.

131. Zero didn't exist in mathematics until the 6th century. It wasn't used in Europe until the 12th century.

132. Between 1984-1992, solo synchronized swimming was an Olympic sport.

133. Gunnar Garfors has traveled to every country in the world. In just over a decade, he set foot in all 198 countries.

134. In 1964, thousands of children scoured Liverpool's Jubilee Park looking for leprechauns. The search went on for over a

month.

135. 10% of Europeans are immune to HIV due to having an ancestor who survived the bubonic plague.

136. Sometimes, rainbows don't have any color. They are known as fogbows.

137. Michael Dacre tried to invent a taxi jet (it's exactly what it sounds like.) He died while testing it.

138. There's a restaurant in Japan called Umkara Ramen Hyouri which pays its customers $438 if they eat their "mega serving" of ramen in less than 20 minutes.

139. The first food to have artificial coloring added to it was butter. Naturally, butter is white.

140. Pepsi was going to be called Brad's Drink.

141. The average prisoner of Alcatraz read about 85 books per year.

142. In certain parts of Britain, if someone has wronged you, you can get on your knees and

shout, "Hear me! Hear me! Come to my aid, my Prince, for someone does me wrong." and then recite the Lord's Prayer in French. If the person wronging you doesn't stop, he must pay a fine.

143. Approximately 4.5 trillion cigarette butts are littered worldwide per year.

144. There is a Russian cruise ship wandering the sea. Nobody resides on it.

145. Water is Fiji's biggest export even though over half of the population have no access to clean water.

146. A doctor in Brazil got so sick of thieves stealing his medical supplies that he covered his fence with HIV-infected syringes and then placed a warning reading "Wall with HIV positive blood. No trespassing."

147. A regular menu can have as many as 185,000 different bacteria on it. Laminated menus have more bacteria than paper ones.

148. It is a custom in China to eat chicken at a funeral to help the dead person's soul fly to heaven.

149. Being repeatedly drunk during Aztec times was a capital crime.

150. A janitor from Chicago wrote a 15,145-page fantasy story with 300 watercolor illustrations. The manuscript was titled In the Realms of the Unreal. Nobody knew it existed until after he died.

151. One of the most elusive counterfeiters in American history was a 72-year-old man called Edward Mueller who made fake $1 bills. He was caught when someone noticed that the bill he was holding misspelt "Washington" as "Wahsington."

152. If a leaky tap drips once per second, it can waste up to 3,000 gallons per year. That's enough water for 180 showers.

153. In 1902, the Saint-Pierre volcano erupted, killing all 35,000 people in town apart from one man. He survived because he was in jail and he was the only prisoner in solitary confinement.

154. Namibia has the oldest reef in the world. It is 548 million years old.

155.	"Demon" means "to divide."

156.	During the Song Dynasty in China, school exams lasted three days nonstop. The exam couldn't be interrupted under any circumstances, even if students died from exhaustion.

157.	When Louis Chevrolet set up his motor company, Chevrolet, he was just a mechanic. By the end of his life, he was... still a mechanic and died bankrupt. His company is currently worth $9.8 billion.

158.	Jack Kilby invented the microchip in 1958. Robert Noyce invented the microchip six months later having no idea that Jack Kilby or his research existed.

159.	Forensic psychologist, Nathan Brooks, studied 261 corporate professionals and concluded that 20% of CEOs are psychopaths. That's a higher rate than in an average prison.

160.	The SkunkLock is a bike lock that shoots a gas if a thief cuts through it. The gas causes the robber to vomit.

161. The "x" in "Xmas" is Greek for "chi" which is the Greek abbreviation of the word "Christ."

162. The first cell phone call was from an engineer called Martin Cooper. He rang a rival engineer to brag about his accomplishment.

163. The chess term "checkmate" is derived from the Persian phrase "Shah Mat" which means "the king is dead."

164. The first automobile in war was the steam car. The British chose it because they could use the boiler to make a cup of tea.

165. In China, it's custom for identical twin sisters who marry identical twin brothers to get plastic surgery so no one gets them mixed up.

166. The King of Jordan is Abdullah bin al-Hussein. He played the Science Division Officer in Star Trek: Voyager. It is his only acting credit.

167. The oldest water in the world resides two

miles below a Canadian mine. The liquid is 2.64 billion years old. That's over half the age of Earth.

168. The ice below the Dry Valleys in Antarctica is the oldest ice in the world. It is 15 million years old.

169. The oldest mountain in the world is Mount Roraima. This Venezuelan mountain is two billion years old.

170. The oldest surface on Earth is the Negev desert in Israel. It has remained unchanged for 1.8 million years. The reason why is because the area has the mildest weather and geological activity in the world, which preserves the region.

171. Basketball legend, Shaquille O' Neal, wears size 22 shoes.

172. Nobody knows who invented donuts or where they were invented or when they were invented.

173. Atsushi Shimizu invented a typhoon turbine that converts wind energy into electricity. Shimizu believes that the power

of a single typhoon could power all of Japan
for half a century.

174. The Rosetta Stone was discovered in 1799
during a Napoleonic campaign in Egypt. The
text on the stone helped us understand the
language of Ancient Egyptians, allowing
archeologists to learn a vast amount about
their culture. The stone is a tax document
written in three languages. Originally, the
stone was used as a wall for a fort.

175. T-Mobile have copyrighted the color
magenta. This might sound absurd but they
have successfully sued other companies
such as Aio Wireless because their logo was
maroon, which was too similar to magenta.

176. In High Wycombe, UK, the mayor is
weighed annually in public and then his
weight is compared to the previous year. If
it has increased, the townspeople see this as
a sign that he has been indulging at the
taxpayer's expense and so the crowd boos
him.

177. Frank Sinatra's son was kidnapped in
1963. The kidnappers said that all
communications must be through

payphones. Sinatra was worried he wouldn't have enough money so he ensured he was carrying a pile of dimes with him at all times. He did this for the rest of his life and was buried with 10 dimes in his pocket.

178. Half a billion years ago, there were 22 hours in a day and over 400 days in a year.

179. There are restrooms in Switzerland lit with blue lights so drug addicts can't see their veins.

180. In the 1800s, people with long beards were believed to be insane. Although Joseph Palmer was mocked, attacked, and stabbed because of his beard, he refused to shave it off. He had a monument of his bearded face on his tombstone, purely out of spite. His grave reads, "Persecuted for wearing the beard."

181. The most lethal earthquake ever occurred in 1556 in Shenshi, China. It killed 830,000 people.

182. There are certain sections of the Pacific Ocean where, if you dug a hole to the opposite point on Earth, you would still be

in the Pacific Ocean.

183. Kublai Khan's niece, Khutulun, said she would marry any suitor if they could defeat her in combat. If they lost, they forfeited their horse. Throughout her life, she won 10,000 horses.

184. Obsidian tools have one of the sharpest natural edges. They are so sharp that they can cut individual cells in half while doing little damage to the surrounding tissue. These blades have been used since the Stone Age.

185. London has so many trees, it can be classified as a forest.

186. Australia has a fusion of hot dogs and hamburgers called Hamdogs.

187. If you are ever near a nuclear blast (which is unlikely) you should avoid using hair conditioner for several weeks, as it will bind radioactive material to your scalp.

188. In 1883, Henry Ziegland broke up with his girlfriend, who then took her own life. The girl's brother tracked down Ziegland and

shot him before committing suicide. Luckily,
Ziegland survived since the bullet only
grazed his head and lodged in a nearby tree.
Years later, Ziegland decided to get rid of
the tree so he blew it up with dynamite. The
explosion propelled the bullet into
Ziegland's skull, killing him.

189.In 1965, a four-year-old almost drowned
at a beach but was rescued by Alice Blaise.
Nine years later, the boy saved a man at the
same beach. That man was Alice Blaise's
husband.

190.In 1974, basketball player, Pete Maravich,
told an interviewer that "I don't want to play
10 years and then die of a heart attack when
I'm 40." He died of a heart attack when he
was 40, after a 10-year career in the NBA.

191.The founder of Match.com is Gary Kreme.
His girlfriend dumped him when she met a
man on Match.com.

192.During the 1930s in Detroit, a baby fell
from a high window and landed on Joseph
Figlock who happened to be passing by.
Figlock and the baby survived the
encounter. A year later, another baby fell

from a window and landed on the same man. Once again, both of them survived. Some sources say that Figlock was struck by the same baby in the second incident but this isn't true.

193. Pantone 448 C is considered to be the world's ugliest color. It looks like a sickly brownish-green. It is used on tobacco products in many European countries.

194. When a missionary told the Amazonian Piraha tribe how his aunt took her own life, the tribe laughed. They had no concept of suicide so they assumed the missionary had told a joke.

195. The Copsey brothers built a jail in California's Lower Lake Stone. They were the first people to be jailed there. They hadn't finished the roof so they escaped, which makes them the first prisoners to escape from the prison.

196. Ancient Egyptian royalty slept with neck supports to preserve their hair.

197. There is a pagoda temple built in 1049 in China that has been hit by 38 earthquakes

and six floods and yet it is still standing.

198. Avocados have more fat than any other fruit or vegetable.

199. The outlaw, Wild Bill, was killed while playing poker. He was holding a pair of aces and eights. This hand is now known as the Dead Man's Hand.

200. There are over 300 billion possible combinations in the first four moves in a game of chess.

201. The concept of a "teenager" didn't exist in most cultures until the 1940s. Before that time, youths were a seen as children until they were 18.

202. Several years ago, a mysterious Polish driver called Prawo Jazdy kept being stopped by police officers in Ireland for speeding. Although he was stopped 50 times over two years, he was never caught because he had 50 different addresses and 50 different dates of birth. He seemed to be a master of disguise, sometimes appearing as a middle-aged man, sometimes as a young woman. After two years, the police

decided to take a Polish police officer on the case to solve the mystery once and for all. When the Pole saw Prawo Jazdy's driver's license, he burst out laughing. He explained that "Prawo Jazdy" means "Driver's license" in Polish, and they had stopped 50 different Polish people, assuming it was the same person.

203. eBay started off as a site that gave information about ebola.

204. Some US hospitals charge $800 for a bag of sterile IV salt water. It only costs $1 to manufacture.

205. It is impossible to tell how many people were killed in the Chernobyl explosion. Some reports claim it was as few as 53 while other sources say it was over 500,000.

206. There are 20 million tons of gold in the ocean.

207. 50 deaf children were put into a school in Nicaragua. Although none of them knew sign language, they created their own version of it. Scientists are researching this to get an idea of how our ancestors

communicated with each other before they had the ability to speak.

208. When the x-ray was discovered, some people thought it was a hoax. The biggest skeptic was Lord Kelvin, who also believed that planes couldn't fly.

209. The most valuable coin is the Flowing Hair US dollar. It was recently sold for $10,016,875.

210. In Rocky II, Rocky runs for over 30 miles in one sprint, which would make him one of the greatest runners in history. This is never mentioned in the series.

211. At the beginning of the millennium, there were 51 billionaires. Now, there are approximately 540 billionaires.

212. KFC used to sell candles that smelled like fried chicken.

213. You may have heard that if a shark is flipped upside down, it will go asleep. Weirdly, orcas know this and use this knowledge to their advantage. When an orca

sees a shark, it will ram the shark in the side
to flip it over so it'll be easier to eat them.

214.   The ocean sunfish lays about 300 million
eggs in one go.

215.When China discovered silk in 2696 BC,
they kept it secret from the rest of the world
for over a thousand years.

216.It's common knowledge that Ancient
Romans watched slaves and soldiers fight
wild animals in the Coliseum. However,
sometimes the activities were a bit more
unorthodox. One activity involved a huge
seesaw called the petaurua. The slaves sat
on it while lions and tigers attacked them.
The objective was to survive by lifting
oneself in the air, which dropped an
opponent to the ground, leaving him
vulnerable. Johnny Knoxville performs this
stunt with bulls in the film, Jackass 2.

217.The bark of the Eucalyptus deglupta tree
is green, yellow, brown, red, orange, and
purple.

218.In 2016, Charlie Lyne released a film
called Paint Drying. The entire film is of a

painted wall drying for 10 hours 7 minutes. He only made it because the British Board of Film Classification must watch every film that has a cinematic release. It was supposed to be 14 hours long but Lyne thought that might be a bit excessive. Soon after it was released, it received a rating of 9.5 on IMDB (Internet Movie Database.) This means that this film was ranked higher than Schindler's List, The Godfather, or Citizen Kane.

219. F1 drivers have their weight monitored more than catwalk models.

220. To save money, nearly every "American" flag in Disneyland has only 37 stars.

221. A malfunctioning slot machine told Katrina Bookman she had won $42.9 million. In reality, she won $2.25.

222. Seismologists don't know what causes tectonic plates to move.

223. Celluloid was invented to replace ivory for making billiard balls.

224. A woman was born with a third

nipple...on her foot.

225. During the Middle Ages, people saved
their money in an orange clay pot called a
pygg. Over time, these became known as
piggy banks.

226.   Ancient Romans believed they could
cure incontinence with the bladder of a
hyena, a roasted seahorse, and boiled mice.

227. Electric eels can jump out of water to
shock predators. The theory that eels can
leap like this has existed since 1800 but was
only proven to be true in 2016.

228. Trees can tell if a deer is trying to eat
them. Trees can detect deer saliva and
produce excess acids which causes its buds
to taste bitter so the deer won't want to eat
them.

229. Scientists at Hiroshima University have
used selective breeding on the glass frog to
give it see-through skin. This makes it easy
to see the frog's muscles, nerves, organs,
and skeleton. This allows biologists to
observe diseases and tumors growing inside
the frog so they can learn more about how

illnesses develop in the body.

230.   The distance a frog can travel is not limited by the power of its back legs but the strength of its front legs since they have to take the brunt of the impact upon landing.

231.   The giraffe has the highest blood pressure in the animal kingdom.

232.Sucralose (modern sweetener) was discovered when a student at King's College misheard "test the compounds" as "taste the compounds."

233.The Chinese invented gunpowder, believing they could turn it into a liquid that would make them immortal.

234.Bras only became popular when, during WWI, there was not enough metal to make corsets.

235.In German folklore, Jesus turned spider webs into tinsel.

236.Iceland is so safe that parents leave babies alone in their strollers while they perform errands.

237.During tests in South Korea, access points to school roofs are locked to prevent students from jumping to their death once they realize they are going to fail their exams.

238.The US dropped 26,171 bombs in 2016. That's an average of three bombs per hour.

239.One of the 13 articles in the 1781 US Articles of Confederation says that Canada can be an America state if it wishes.

240.In 1831, Pope Gregory XVI banned gas lights in Papal states and wanted them to be banned worldwide because God established the delincation between night and day and altering this defied God's law.

241.Alice Cooper believes everything that is written in the Old Testament (including the part that says bats are birds.)

242.Eminem banned swearing in his house.

243.The King of Hearts is the only king in a deck of playing cards that doesn't have a moustache.

244. Somebody once wrote this on the website,
4chan –
"Art used to be something to cherish
Now literally anything could be art.
This post is art."
This post was printed, framed and sold on
eBay for $90,900.

245. The Laetiporus mushroom tastes like fried
chicken.

246. The Corryvreckan Maelstrom is a Scottish
whirlpool that has been spinning for 1,400
years.

247. A boulevard is a wide street with trees on
both sides. A lane is a narrow, rural road. A
drive is a long, winding, scenic road.

248. Pierre Cota got into a car crash and a
plane crash...in the same day. The car crash
caused a pile-up and the plane crash killed
87 people. Not only did Cota survive both
incidents but he went to work immediately
after. He wasn't even late.

249. During the 1800s at Christmas time, Santa
wrote to children instead of the other way

around. Santa told kids what naughty things they needed to stop doing to guarantee they would receive presents. Santa even gave specific examples e.g. you broke a vase, hit your sibling, stole a biscuit, etc. to prove that Santa is always watching.

250. An attacker sent a bright flashing GIF via Twitter to an epileptic called Kurt Eichenwald after Eichenwald criticized Trump. When Eichenwald opened the file, he had a seizure. The attacker was aware Eichenwald suffered seizures and wrote "YOU DESERVE A SEIZURE FOR YOUR POSTS" in the GIF. This may be the first time in history where a GIF was sent to trigger a person's epilepsy.

251. In medieval times, Christians abstained from eating eggs during Lent. When Lent ended, there was a surplus of eggs which is why they are associated with Easter.

252. Conventional Christmas trees are evergreen fir. Although they have been used for millennia for winter festivals, they have only been used for Christmas for the last thousand years. Originally, they hung upside down from the ceiling.

253. Irish jack o' lanterns were carved in turnips (not pumpkins) to ward off an evil spirit called Jack.

254. Samsung has 275,000 employees. That's more than Google, Apple and Microsoft combined.

255. Samsung sells oil tankers.

256. The three most recognizable scents are coffee, peanut butter, and crayons.

257. John Shepherd Barron and Don Wetzel invented the ATM one year apart even though they didn't know the other existed.

258. New Years was first celebrated by the Babylonians 4,000 years ago.

259. By law, homeopathy treatments require print warnings on their labels stating that there is no scientific evidence that they work.

260. British people spend $50 million on astrology per year.

261.A YouTuber called Yaog used a drone to prove his wife was cheating on him. You can watch the video that the drone took online.

262.The Coca-Cola logo is recognized by 94% of the world's population.

263.As of October 2015, Google has acquired 184 companies including Motorola and YouTube. Google spent over $28 billion on these acquisitions.

264.Wal-Mart has 2.3 million employees.

265.Little Red Riding Hood's name is Blanchette.

266.Disneyland Resort has 800 species of plants which are indigenous to 40 nations, making it one of the most diverse botanical locales in the western United States.

267.Coca-Cola makes $43 billion per year.

268.McDonalds serves nine million pounds of fries per day.

269.1% of all the commercial wood in the world is used by IKEA.

270. There are some conspiracy theorists including David Icke who believe the Moon isn't real.

271. Many important people in the Bible are unnamed including Noah's wife, Cain's wife, the criminals crucified with Christ, the soldier who pierced Christ's side, and the Wise Men.

272. There are many techniques that psychics use for their fortune-telling. Tarot cards, crystal balls, tea leaves, bread...wait...what? That's right. In ancient times, bread-reading (alphitomancy) was used by fortune tellers. And it wasn't used just as a parlor trick. It was used to catch criminals. Suspects were rounded up and given a piece of bread. Whoever thought the bread tasted bad was seen as the true criminal.

273. The Museum of Non-Visible Art is a museum with...no art. If that sounds stupid, Aimee Davison bought a piece of this Non-Existent Art for $10,000. This museum was set up by the actor, James Franco.

274. Although Norse mythology sounds like an

ancient religion, there are some people who still worship the Norse gods, Thor and Odin. They belong to a church called Asatruarfelagid.

275.In 1964, Donald Currey cut down a tree to see how old it was. Upon researching the specimen, he learned it was over 5,000 years old. At the time, it was the oldest tree ever found and is, to this date, the second oldest tree ever discovered...and Currey killed it out of curiosity.

276.Shridhar Chillal has the longest fingernail ever. His thumbnail measured 77.87 inches.

277.Charles Byrne is the most famous giant in Irish history standing 7ft 7. He was terrified that his body would be put on display after he died and he begged to be buried at sea. He wanted weights on his coffin so no one could bring his body up to the surface. When he died, his corpse was stolen by his former housemate. He was dissected and his skeleton was put on display. It can still be seen today in the Hunterian Museum at the Royal College of Surgeons of England.

278.Mary Bach sued Wal-Mart for 2¢ and won.

279. The color mauve was created by accident while doctors were trying to treat malaria. In 1856, William Perkin attempted to engineer a cheap, effective way to simulate quinine; a substance to treat malaria. Although the material failed, Perkin noticed that the quinine turned a unique shade of purple and marketed it for fashion.

280. WC Roentgen discovered x-rays in 1895. He called it "x-ray" because "x" meant "unknown" and he had no idea what he had discovered. The first x-ray was of his wife's hand. When he saw it, he said, "I have seen my death."

281. X-rays were used to promote shoe ads.

282. 12th century judges in China used to cover their eyes to hide their expressions in court.

283. The Heimlich maneuver doesn't work if a person is choking on Jell-O.

284. Modern matches were created by accident.

285. In the 1800s, headphones weighed up to

11lbs. That's almost as heavy as a human head.

286.The Aztecs invented popcorn to decorate headdresses and necklaces.

287.Legend states that Rome was founded by Romulus. The first emperor of Rome was Augustus. The last emperor of Rome was called Romulus Augustus.

288.Christine Maggiore was an AIDS skeptic and wrote a book called What If Everything You Thought You Knew About AIDS Was Wrong?
She died of AIDS.

289."Amen" means "so be it."

290.94% of Chinese live in the east side of the country.

291.In July 1974, Neville Ebbin was killed by a taxi while riding his moped on a Bermuda street. The following July, his brother Erskine was killed by the same taxi driver, on the same street, driving the same moped, and carrying the same passenger. Both Neville and Erskine died when they were 17.

292. Sumo wrestlers are not allowed to drive.

293. The bacteria on television remote can survive for over two days.

294. Cabbage, cauliflower, broccoli, kale, and Brussel sprouts are technically the same food. They are genetic modifications of wild cabbage. In its original state, this cabbage looks like a small yellow flower.

295. Field crickets chirp to attract females. If a cricket can't get laid, they may become desperate and chirp so often, they die from exhaustion.

296. Rats can chew through cement and brick.

297. Ancient Romans chose puppies by surrounding a litter with an oil-soaked string and setting it on fire. The Romans believed the dogs' mother saved them in the order of preference.

298. When the penduline tit is about to lay her eggs, she will hide from her partner. After she lays the eggs, she will abandon them, forcing the male to care for the chicks.

299.When airplanes started to become popular, very few people could afford to fly. This made the airline market incredibly competitive and airlines served a diverse menu of full meals. Alcohol was free and unlimited.

300.You may wonder why eggplants are so called when they clearly don't look like eggs. Well, 500 years ago, they did. Due to centuries of genetic modification and selective breeding, they took on an oblong shape and purple color.

301.The X, W, and Q Scrabble tiles were banned in Turkey for 90 years. The ban was lifted in 2013.
  The entire game was banned in Romania until the 1980s for being "overly intellectual."

302.Japanese is the hardest language for an English-speaking person to learn.

303.The majority of ninjas were women. Women were not allowed to be samurai so many chose to be ninjas instead.

304.The axe was invented in Australia
approximately 49,000 years ago.

305.Drugs aren't illegal in Portugal. If you are
caught with heroin, cocaine or crystal meth,
you may be sent to a counselor but you
won't go to jail.

306.In a deck of cards, the Hearts represent
the church, Spades represent the military,
Clubs represent agriculture and Diamonds
represent merchants.

307.The ocean contains enough uranium to
power the planet for 10,000 years.

308.According to Tim Darling, the best
properties to buy in Monopoly are The
Railroads, then the orange properties, and
then the light blue properties.

309.Japanese toilets play music to drown out
unpleasant noises.

310.During a hurricane storm, Matt Suter was
hurled the equivalent of three football fields.
He survived with no injuries apart from a
cut on his forehead. He has the world record
for longest distance traveled by tornado.

311. If you are 20 inches away from someone in a dark room while they have a candle lit behind them, their face will become distorted and appear demonic. According to Italian psychologist, Giovanni Caputo, this is because in impaired light, the brain can't bind all the facial elements into a single image.

312. If you drink ayahuasca, you will experience intense hallucinations but you will be fully aware that the images you see are not real.

313. Burger King had a promotion where you won a free Whopper if you unfriended ten people on Facebook. The application alerted your former friends that they had been unfriended for a Whopper.

314. Most people believe the Notification Globe symbol on Facebook always looks the same. However, its appearance is based on where in the world you are when you log in.

315. Thomas Fitzpatrick told one of his friends that he had got drunk two years earlier and landed a plane in the middle of Manhattan,

in front of a bar When his friend didn't
believe him, Fitzpatrick did it again.

316. There is a Banyan tree in Pakistan that has
been under arrest for over a century. It is
tied to the ground with chains.

317. Per calorie, broccoli has more protein than
beef.

318. Ask one of your friends the following four
questions –
What's 1+4?
What's 2+5?
What's 7-3?
Can you name a vegetable?
For some reason, 90% answer the fourth
question with "carrot."

319. There used to be a No-Nose Club for
noseless people in England during the 19th
century.

320. A professor of Egyptology called Nabir
Al-Sammund believes the pyramids were
built by dinosaurs.
Some people don't believe this.

321.   There is a cave in Romania where the atmosphere is composed of sulfur, making it lethal to humans. However, 33 species have adapted to the atmosphere and thrive in this cave. These creatures don't exist anywhere else in the world.

322.   Despite the fact that a zebra shark was alone for four years in an Australian aquarium, it gave birth to three babies. When the offspring were tested, they only had the DNA of their mother.

323.   Monkeys do not have a specific technique to swing from trees. They each have their own style, which means they have to teach themselves how to move through the trees.

324. A mole can dig 300ft in one night.

325. Pearls melt in vinegar.

326. There is a mushroom called Chorioactis that is only found in two places on Earth – Texas and Japan; 6,800 miles apart.

327. If you type "Do the harlem shake" into YouTube, the YouTube symbol will start

dancing.

328.If you type "Use the force luke" into
YouTube, the search results start hovering
as if they are being moved by the Force.

329.The letters J and K are not used for any
number (one, two, three, hundred,
thousand, million, billion, trillion,
googolplex, sextillion, vigintiliion, etc.)

330.Until the first century BC, it was legal for a
father in Ancient Rome to kill anyone in his
family for any reason. He held onto this
right until the day he died.

331.An Easter egg is a secret hidden in a
computer code (Internet, video game, DVD,
etc.). If you type "Easter Egg (media)" into
the search bar on Wikipedia, a picture of
rabbits will appear with the accompanying
article. In the bottom right of this picture is
a hedgehog. If you hover around the
hedgehog, the text, "I'm a hedgehog, not an
egg!" appears. If you click on the hedgehog,
a picture of Easter eggs appear.

332.It was illegal for an Ancient Roman to be
buried if they had been killed by lightning as

it was "stealing a sacrifice from Jupiter."

333.The song, Jimmy Crack Corn, is about a
slave celebrating the death of his master.

334.In Ancient Rome, people were paid to cry
at funerals to make the recently deceased
seem more loved and respected. However,
some people went overboard with their
performance and scratched their faces and
tore their hair out. It got so bad that crying
was outlawed at funerals.

335.Wearing purple was illegal in Ancient
Rome.

336.The song, Frere Jacques, was created to
mock Jews.

337.William Buckland is known as the Man
Who Ate Everything. He tried to eat every
type of animal possible including bats,
alligators, mice and even humans. He said
the only animal he didn't like to eat was the
mole.

338.There are parking spaces in Seoul, South
Korea that are only to be used by women.
The spots are painted pink.

339. A British man had a typo on his plane ticket. He changed his name and got a new passport since it was cheaper than paying the airline the name-change fee.

340. The oldest mask ever found is 9,000 years old.

341. Japanese subways are so busy, people are employed to shove travelers into crowded trains.

342. After Nazi Germany surrendered, Russia celebrated so intensely that they ran out of vodka after one day.

343. 60% of all the world's Christmas decorations are made in a Chinese town called Yiwu.

344. The 1994 comedy, Baby's Day Out, is as popular in India as Star Wars is in the Western world. It's been remade twice in India. For some reason, the second remake is called James Bond.

345. The Terracotta Army in China was discovered in 1974 by farmers while they

were digging a well.

346. India suffers more deadly traffic accidents
than any other country. The World Health
Organization (WHO) recorded 105,725 fatal
traffic accidents in 2009. However, since
there are over a billion people in India, the
WHO assumes that there are almost as
many lethal accidents that go unreported.
This means that there are about 200,000
deaths involving traffic in India every year.
By comparison, around 42,600 people die in
the US in traffic accidents annually. If a
driver in India kills a homeless person with
their car, the driver will rarely lose his or
her license. If a driver kills a child by
crashing into them, they will only be fined
$780 and face one year in prison.

347. Tom Cruise dated Cher.

348. Beach holidays only became popular in
the 18th century.

349. After Hurricane Katrina, Cuba and
Venezuela offered mobile hospitals, water
treatment plants, canned food, bottled
water, over a thousand doctors, more than
25 metric tons of medicine, heating oil and

$1 million in aid. The US government rejected them.

350. Most criminals who were executed via guillotine didn't know the day of their death until 30 minutes prior.

351.   The greater flamingo is worse at relationships than any other bird. 99% of their relationships end with one of the flamingos cheating on its partner or abandoning him or her.

352.   Certain birds like black kites and brown falcons know how to start fires. In 2016, these birds were spotted in Australia picking up burning twigs and dropping them in other places so animals would run out into the open, making them easier to catch.

353. A cavefish from Thailand has been spotted walking and climbing waterfalls like a salamander.

354. Coyotes and badgers hunt together. The badger digs up the prey and the coyote chases it.

355. A guy made a chicken sandwich from scratch. Literally. He grew wheat in his garden, then harvested and milled it, killed a chicken, boiled water that he obtained from the ocean, etc. It took him six months and cost $1,500. When he finally ate his very own chicken sandwich, he said it tasted awful.

356. A conlanger is a person who is employed to invent languages. Dr. Paul Frommer is a conlanger and devised the Na'vi dialect in the film, Avatar.

357. The director of The Hangover trilogy, Todd Philips, had his first film funded by John Wayne Gacy; a serial killer who murdered over 30 people.

358. The eye drops, Chlorin e6, give the user night-vision.

359. The most expensive thing ever sold on eBay was a jet for $4.9 million.

360. A woman in Georgia was looking for copper with a metal detector and accidentally cut a cable. This led to the entire nation of Armenia losing their

Internet for five hours.

361. The first Olympic champion was Korobus the cook.

362. Pink Floyd, Led Zeppelin, Genesis, Elton John, and two of the Beatles funded the Monty Python films.

363. Canada consumes more donuts than any other country.

364. MySpace had two chances to buy Facebook.

365. When Brazil lost the 1950 World Cup in their own country, three Brazilian fans in the stadium died from heart attacks and one committed suicide out of shame.

366. The US government provides up to 300 pre-rolled marijuana joints per months to each of the four surviving patients from an abandoned medical program from 1976.

367. In the1850s, communication between the US and the UK took 17 hours.

368. It is common knowledge that the athletes

in the Ancient Olympics were naked.
However, few people know that their
coaches were naked too.

369.It is illegal to frown in Milan, Italy except
in hospitals and at funerals.

370.The modern Olympics have only been
canceled once due to war.

371.In the 1980s, a mobile phone took 10
hours to charge and would only last for a
30-minute conversation. It cost $4,000.

372.In China, "Kan ye" means "someone who
brags a lot with no actions to follow it up."

373.Oetzi "The Iceman" is a 5,300-year-old
mummy that was discovered in the Alps in
1991. In the next 13 years, seven people
connected to Oetzi's discovery died. The
mummy's examiner, Konrad Spindler, died
the same year that Oetzi was excavated. The
discoverer, Helmut Simon, died in a blizzard
accident not too far away from where Oetzi
was found. When Simon died, Oetzi's
archeologist, Tom Loy stated, "I think it's a
load of rubbish. It's all a media hype. The
next thing you will be saying I will be next."

He died that same year.

374. Route 66 was a TV show in the 1960s that followed the adventures of two drifters journeying through America. The episode, I'm Here to Kill a King, was supposed to be aired on November 29th 1963. It was canceled because the story was too similar to the assassination of John F. Kennedy, which had happened only one week earlier. In the episode, the two main characters meet a man who looks exactly like one of the lead characters. This man intends to kill an Arab king. This king travels through the streets in an automobile in a similar fashion to JFK. The shooter tries to take the king out from a grassy knoll. Over 50 witnesses of JFK's murder stated that they heard gunshots come from a grassy knoll. Both targets were to be shot in the head. JFK's assassin was Lee Harvey Oswald. One of the characters in the episode is called Lee. JFK was assassinated in Dallas. In this episode, the characters consider hiding out in Dallas. One of the characters says that he's going to "Fritz's for lunch." Fritz was the name of the police officer who interrogated Oswald. Everyone knows the JFK assassination has spawned many conspiracy theories. This

episode's story revolves around a conspiracy since the king's assassination is organized by his own head of security.

375. The first text message read, "Merry Christmas."

376. Lightning can be as hot as 30,000 degrees Celsius. That's five times hotter than the surface of the Sun.

377. There are more collect calls on Father's Day than any other day.

378. Michael Jordan makes more in a single year nowadays than he did in his entire 15-year career in the NBA.

379. In 2016, Luke Aikins set a world record by jumping from a height of 25,000ft into a net without a parachute. The stunt was broadcast on television with a five-second-delay, just in case anything went wrong. He landed in the net without suffering any injuries.

380. It's not uncommon for citizens of Iceland to draw out maps for others to get to locations, even if they don't know the name

of the place they wish to visit. In fact, some people find the towns names unhelpful since they are so hard to spell and pronounce.

381. You can legally drive a tank in England, even if you are using the vehicle to drive to the shop.

382. During World War II, the US considered dyeing Mt Fuji black as a psychological tactic against the Japanese.

383. Toy globes were banned in India until 2004.

384. There is a thermometer that looks like a leaf. It turns brown if the room temperature drops below 20 degrees Celsius and yellow if it raises above 25 degrees Celsius.

385. There is a theme park in Lithuania that recreates life as a USSR citizen. Each visitor has their belongings confiscated, is given a gas mask, experiences an interrogation and must learn the Soviet anthem. If you get through all of this, you receive a shot of vodka.

386. The average person spends six months of their life waiting for a red light to turn green.

387. It is illegal to name your child "5th" in New Zealand.

388. There's a Japanese town that has 34 recycling categories.

389. The US federal government can legally read emails of any citizen if the emails are over 180 days old.

390. SpreadThat! is a self-heating butter knife that harnesses the warmth of your body by using thermal conductive titanium.

391. Women are more likely to suffer from nightmares and insomnia. Studies have been done on both adults and children across the world and the results have almost always been the same.

392. A 1910 book series revolved around a boy-inventor called Tom Swift. The book, Tom Swift and His Electric Rifle inspired the invention of the taser. The word "taser" is derived from "Tom A. Swift Electric Rifle."

393.In Japan, it is considered good luck for a
sumo wrestler to make a baby cry.

394.Most people are familiar with The Three
Wise Monkeys – See No Evil, Hear No Evil,
Speak No Evil. Few people are aware that
there is another monkey that represents Do
No Evil.

395.   Octopuses are left-eyed or right-eyed
much like how a person is left-handed or
right-handed.

396.Most female animals have two ovaries.
However, female chickens have one ovary
and a proto-testicle. If a chicken becomes so
ill that it risks its ovary being damaged, it
may turn into a male to protect itself. This
means that female chickens can turn
themselves into males by growing a set of
testicles. However, males can't convert to
females.

397.In 2011, a chicken stabbed a man to death.
I know that sounds ridiculous so I'd better
explain. During a cockfight, Jose Luis Ochoa
was cut in the thigh by a rooster that was
equipped with a blade in its talons. Ochoa

died in the hospital soon after.

398.   Prairie dogs can communicate the size,
color and speed of a human to other prairie
dogs in $1/10^{th}$ of a second.

399. In 1971, burglars stole records from the
FBI by leaving a note on the front door of
their Delaware office reading "Please don't
lock this door tonight."

400. Benedict XI was the pope three times.

401. Heribert Illig is a historian who genuinely
believes that the entire Medieval era (600-
900 AD) didn't happened.

402. There are five temples in Kyoto, Japan that
have blood-stained ceilings. The ceilings are
made from the floorboards of a castle where
warriors killed themselves after being
cornered by the enemy. You can see the
outlines of their footprints in these ceilings.

403. Although the Bubonic Plague was the
worst plague in European history, there
were 16 plagues in London between 1348
and 1665.

404. By 2080, the human population of Earth is expected to be 10.8 billion.

405. The average person breathes 8.4 million times a year.

406. Over 60,000 people are flying over the US right now.

407. At least 150 people are killed by coconuts annually.

408. 50% of people in the United States claim to be on a diet at any one time.

409. The average Slinky measures 87ft long if it is stretched out.

410. There are several emojis that reference Kim Kardashian.

411. One cloud can weigh over 500 tons.

412. In 1902, Leon Teisserence de Bort discovered the Earth's stratosphere. Richard Assmann discovered it independently three days later.

413. In 2006, a page on the Chevy website

allowed people to make their own car commercial to advertise the release of the Chevrolet Tahoe. However, countless pranksters had fun with the site and made the most inappropriate ads possible by including captions like "Don't Buy Me" and "Murder Your Entire Family" before Chevy shut it down.

414. The first aerial refueling happened in 1921 when Wesley May carried a five-gallon can of gasoline on his back whilst climbing from one plane to another.

415. Although women are far more inclined to suffer illnesses than men, women live longer.

416. Napping at work is considered a good sign in Japan as it shows employees are working for hours on end.

417. It's illegal to name your child Osama Bin Laden or Adolf Hitler in Germany.

418. Mike Tyson started taking cocaine when he was 11.

419. Hatebeak is a black metal band whose

lead singer is a parrot.

420. In Greek and Roman cultures, suicide was seen as a heroic act.

421. A 23-year-old con-artist called Frederic Bourdin assumed the identity of a 16-year-old Texan boy. The family wanted to believe he was their lost son so much, that they went along with it for months, even though he had a French accent, was seven years too old, and had different colored eyes.

422. Heinrich Himmler was the leading member of the Nazi SS. He almost fainted when he saw Jews being executed. He was the one who gave the order to execute them.

423. Anette Jeffreys had £17,500 stolen from her bank account. Her bank refunded her 10p.

424. The idea that an author owns the rights to their own stories didn't exist until 1710. This is why William Shakespeare was able to copy so many other stories without suffering legal consequences.

425. It's harder to diagnose autism in girls

because they have fewer repetitive behaviors, their hobbies tend to be more socially acceptable, and they normally have a superior vocabulary.

426. Emo fashion has been illegal in Russia since 2008.

427. In 1961, Leonid Rogozov's appendix burst. With no one else around, he surgically removed his own appendix.

428.   During World War II, 75,000 British troops suffered "trench foot." This is a swelling in the foot caused by cold and persistent damp in the trenches. To prevent this, Edgar Ellington tried to invent a waterproof sock. However, his invention kept bursting when too much water got in.
   He realized that these "water grenades" would sell better as a children's toy. Eventually, they became better known as water balloons.

429. The most dangerous steps on a staircase are the bottom two and the top two.

430. The Honduran White Bat is one of the only bats that doesn't live in a cave. Instead, it

lives in the leaves of the rainforest.

431. According to the book, Comprehensive Asian Fighting Arts, ninjas have used gliders in combat. But that's not the weirdest thing they have done. During one siege, ninjas built a yagura, which worked like a rudimentary Ferris wheel, and brought ninjas up over steep walls so quickly, it was described as "a stream."

432. Norway, Switzerland, France, and Chile don't recognize Scientology as a religion.

433. An Auschwitz prisoner called Kazimierz Piechoski escaped with three others from the death camp by dressing up as Nazis and stealing the Deputy Fuhrer's car. When Piechoski's group were stopped at the gate, Piechoski barked orders until the guards backed off and let them escape.

434. Sicilian students invented a vending machine that turns trash into phone cases.

435. Lululemon is a Canadian athletic clothing retailer. Its founder came up with the name because he thought it would be funny watching Japanese people try to pronounce

it.

436. Oxford University is home to a battery-powered bell that's been ringing since 1840. No one knows what the battery is made of but nobody wants to open it to find out in case they can't put it back together. We won't know how it works until it stops and scientists are allowed to take it apart.

437. Originally, a moment was 90 seconds long.

438. Dice are slightly more likely to land showing the number on top after they are rolled.

439. In Soviet Russia, there were two newspapers; Pravda (which means "Truth") and Izvestia (which means "News.") The Russians joked, "There is no truth in the News and there is no news in the Truth."

440. Reading became so commonplace in the 1700s, society panicked that young people (especially women) were suffering from "reading rage," "reading fever," reading mania" and "reading lust."

441. Emma Morano is the last person on Earth

to be born in the 19th century.

442. Australia is the only continent whose people never independently created the bow and arrow.

443. Regardless of country, age, or culture, women tend to sleep 19 minutes longer than men on average.

444. The US government gave Indiana University $1 million to study memes.

445. The Russian version of Who Wants to be a Millionaire? had to remove the Ask the Audience lifeline since the audience intentionally gave the wrong answers.

446. The hacktivist group, Anonymous, sent thousands of all-black faxes to the Church of Scientology to deplete their ink cartridges.

447. In the 1950s, CIA agents tied their shoelaces a certain way to give secret messages. One shoelace pattern meant "Follow me" while another meant "I have brought someone."

448. Elephants can tell the difference between

human languages and know which speech pattern belong to people with a history of hurting and killing elephants.

449.There is a rock formation on Iceland's coast that looks like an elephant.

450.FedEx keeps multiple empty cargo planes in the skies overnight on circuitous flight paths, ready to change their path to accommodate unexpected package volume.

451.A Coca-Cola employee can get fired for drinking Pepsi on the job.

452.Originally, the American flag salute was the same as the Nazi salute. It was changed in 1942.

453.The United Arab Emirates is strongly considering building a mountain to try and change its climate.

454.There is a secret room at the top of the Eiffel Tower that was assigned to the creator, Gustave Eiffel.

455.In the film, 300, Leonidas and his Spartans fight in the battle of Thermopylae. Although

Leonidas was real, he was 60 years old at the time of the battle.

456. Rose Davies was raised by foster parents and was only told later in life that she had three brothers. Although she tracked down two of her siblings, Sid and John, her third brother, Chris, was much more elusive. After years of searching, she found Chris in the house across from hers.

457. The Carpathia ship rescued Titanic survivors. It later sunk.

458. Morgan Robertson wrote a book called Futility, or the Wreck of the Titan. It revolved around a ship which sank even though it had a reputation for being unsinkable. It was written 14 years before the Titanic sunk.

459. There was supposed to be a lifeboat drill on the Titanic the same day it sank.

460. In 1809, the Spanish town of Huescar declared war on Denmark. Then they forgot about it for 172 years. No shots were fired and no one died in the war. In 1981, a historian randomly discovered the

declaration and a peace treaty had to be signed to end the "war."

461. Facial hair was popular in the US until WWI because it was easier to secure a gas mask to clean-shaven skin.

462. Shemika Charles is the greatest limbo dancer in the world. She can limbo under a car.

463. The first thing ever written on the Internet was "lo." It was supposed to say "login" but the computer crashed after the first two letters.

464. Steven Jay Russell was a prisoner who walked out of jail by pretending to be a prison guard. When he was recaptured, he paid his bail by pretending to be the judge. When he was caught again, he walked out of prison by pretending to be a doctor. When he was captured AGAIN, he got out AGAIN by pretending to be dead.

465. Beyoncé used to sing while running a mile so she could get used to performing on stage while being exhausted.

466. The Sandbox Tree is covered in spikes. Each spike is poisonous. If one of these spikes is penetrated, the fruit inside will explode. This plant is nicknamed the Dynamite Tree.

467. During the Iranian Embassy Siege, the hostages were asked which of them should be released. Most of them chose a man whose snoring kept them awake.

468. Vlado Taneski was a real-life Dexter; he was a serial killer who also worked as a crime reporter. He reported on his own crimes and was only caught after he wrote articles on murders that were not yet publicly known.

469. A law professor called Roger Fisher suggested that the nuclear launch codes be implanted in a volunteer's heart. He said the president should kill the innocent person with a butcher's knife to get the codes. Fisher hypothesized that if the president felt he couldn't physically take a human life, he shouldn't make a decision that would take the lives of hundreds of thousands of people.

470. In 1994, LA police officers arrested a man who was dressed as the Grim Reaper and brandishing a scythe while hanging around outside old people's houses.

471. Nuclear bombs have made it much easier to detect fake art. (Bear with me on this one.) Nuclear explosions release isotopes called Strontium-90 and cesium-137. These isotopes did not exist prior to their release in nuclear explosions – the earliest of which took place in 1945. If a piece of artwork contains these elements but purports to be older than 1945, it's a forgery.

472. There are "your mother" jokes in the Bible.

473. Guillotine executions used to attract crowds of up to 30,000 people.

474. Nearly every arcade has a claw machine. Most claw machines are programmed to only give the claw full strength 5% of the time.

475. There is a plant in China and Japan called Physalis alkekengi which is a symbol of "life within death." It blooms in the winter and

dries up in the spring, revealing the fruit that lives inside it, which resembles a heart inside a ribcage.

476. Adidas will cancel their sponsorship of any sportsperson who is affiliated with Scientology.

477. There's a boiling lake in Dominica that is too hot to enter. As a result, no one knows how deep it is.

478. Creative Room Engineering will create hidden rooms in your home that can be opened by performing a specific combination on a chess board.

479. The Civil War epic, Gone with the Wind, is considered to be one of the greatest films ever made. Ironically, it gets the date of the Civil War wrong. In the film, the War ended on April 9th 1865. In reality, it ended on May 26th.

480. England took part in the shortest war in history when they battled Zanzibar. Zanzibar admitted defeat after 38 minutes.

481. You need to chew gum for 18 hours to

burn off 200 calories.

482. You need to apply lip balm 750 times to burn off 100 calories.

483. Alexander Bogdanov was a Russian scientist who believed he could become immortal by transfusing himself with the blood from other people. He died after transfusing the blood of a student who suffered malaria. Weirdly, the student made a complete recovery.

484. Although 71 people witnessed Robert McCartney murder a man in Belfast, all of them told the police that they saw nothing because they were in the bathroom. The police nicknamed this bathroom "the TARDIS."

485. Soccer legend, Ronaldinho Gaucho, became a media sensation at 13 years old when his team won 23-0. He scored every goal.

486. Although it's easy to get stuck in quicksand, it's difficult to sink because the fluid is twice as thick as water. Once half of your body becomes stuck, you won't sink

any further if you don't wriggle.

487. The Ouija Board is named after the French and German words for "yes" – "oui" and "ja."

488. The King of Morocco, Hassan II, was the subject of an assassination attempt. During the attack, he grabbed a radio and told the rebels who were shooting at his plane, "Stop firing! The tyrant is dead!" This made the assassins cease their attack.

489. The US Constitution, the Declaration of Independence, and the Bill of Rights are lowered into a bomb-proof safe every night.

490. Owning a Bible only became commonplace in the 1600s; nearly 1300 years after the Bible was written.

491. #KardBlock is an app that disables all mentions of the Kardashians online.

492. The Chinese word for "contradiction" loosely translates into "spear shield." It is derived from an old Chinese story of a merchant who claimed to sell spears that could pierce any shield and shields that could withstand any spear.

493. Hard drugs are so rare in Japan, that the country faced an epidemic in the mid-1980s when the number of suspected heroin users skyrocketed from 29 to 36.

494. The blobfish is considered to be the ugliest animal in the world.

495. Nine-banded armadillos suffer from Hansen's disease (which is often mistaken for leprosy.) However, armadillos in Florida are immune to Hansen's.

496. You can buy dinosaur excrement for a few thousand dollars. It's called coprolite.

497. North American beavers used to be larger than cars.

498. Before the invention of fridges, Russians dropped frogs in their milk to keep it fresh. You know what's even weirder? It worked. Secretions in the amphibians' skin contain antimicrobial compounds called peptides which are effective against salmonella.

499. 60% of all animation comes from Japan.

500. Cliff Curtis is an actor who has played a terrorist more times than almost any actor. He played a Colombian terrorist leader in Collateral Damage, an Iraqi rebel in Three Kings, a Latino gangster in Training Day, and a druglord in Blow. Curtis is from New Zealand.

501. Lead actor and writer of Curb Your Enthusiasm, Larry David, has never owned a camera. In fact, he's never taken a photograph in his entire life.

502. Dr. Thomas Midgley has caused more damage to the Earth's atmosphere than any other person, because he is personally responsible for adding lead to fuel and for creating chlorofluorocarbons in refrigerators.

503. Theophilus Van Kannel invented the revolving door. He only created it because he didn't like the idea of opening a door for a woman.

504. An island in-between Australia and New Caledonia has appeared on maps for over a century. Recently, scientists learned that this island doesn't exist.

505. Rapper, Tupac Shakur, was supposed to play a Jedi in Star Wars: Episode I – The Phantom Menace, but he died before production began.

506. Several years ago, it took 12 months to sell 10 million iPhones. Nowadays, Apple sells 10 million iPhones in two days.

507. Legendary director, Stanley Kubrick, received a fan letter from Akira Kurosawa, who is often considered to be the greatest film director of all time. Kubrick believed he shouldn't write back unless he had the perfect reply. He obsessed for months and months and wrote many unsent drafts for a response. Sadly, Kurosawa died before Kubrick sent a reply.

508. In most movies, the heroes appear from the left and the villains appear from the right. If a hero regularly enters from the right, it usually means they will eventually turn bad or they are secretly evil.

509. Legendary sprinter, Jesse Owens, used to race against dogs and horses to prepare for the Olympics.

510. A lifeguard from South Florida saved a person from drowning. The lifeguard was fired because the woman he saved wasn't drowning in his designated section.

511. If the entire Internet crashed, there are seven people in the world who have keycards to reboot the system. A reboot requires the simultaneous operation of five of the keys.

512. Alfred Binet devised the IQ test. He hated the fact that it was used to highlight who was smart, since he only created it to identify struggling students.

513. There is no point in The Lord of the Rings films where two female characters speak to each other.

514. Although the Chinese invented fireworks, the Italians made fireworks the way we know them today. Italians used calcium to make them orange, sodium to make them yellow, and barium to make them green. They used cylindrical tubes to make them whistle, aluminum flakes to make them hiss and flash powder to make them echo.

515. In 1914, a British WWI soldier called Thomas Hughes wrote a letter to his wife and then tossed it into the English Channel, just days before he died. 85 years later, the letter was found in the River Thames and given to his wife's 86-year-old daughter.

516. The Philippines restaurant, Isdaan Floating Restaurant, allows you to smash plates to vent your anger.

517. Scientists have recently learned how to unboil egg whites.

518. George Lalonde performed the first Saw-a-Person-in-Half magic trick in 1936 in Quebec. Since the trick had never been done before, the audience genuinely believed that Lalonde was going to chop his assistant in two. An audience member called Henry Howard ran onstage and stabbed the magician in the back to rescue his assistant. Lalonde suffered a collapsed lung but later recovered.

519. The 1895 film, The Execution of Mary Stuart, is the first movie with a special effect. In one scene, a woman is decapitated

with a sword. A special effect is used so the soon-to-be headless woman is edited out of the shot and replaced with a mannequin moments before she is decapitated. The clip is only 18 seconds long.

520. The 1922 film, The Toll of the Sea, was the first color film in Hollywood.

521. The 1973 film, Westworld, was the first movie with computer effects.

522. The 1917 cartoon, Namakura Gatana, was the first anime ever.

523. The 1888 film, Roundhay Garden Scene, was the first film ever made.

524. The first digitally shot feature film was Julia and Julia in 1987.

525. The first film to have a trailer was The Pleasure Seekers in 1913.

526. The first computer generated character was in the 1981 film, Looker.

527. The 1929 film, Hearts in Dixie, was the first Hollywood movie with an all-black cast.

528. Over 90% of American films made before 1929 no longer exist.

529.The 1976 film, A Star is Born, was the first film to use Dolby Stereo Sound.

530.The terraforming scene in Star Trek II: The Wrath of Khan is the first scene that was entirely computer-generated.

531.The first PG-13 film in the US was Red Dawn, which was released in 1984.

532.The 2004 film, Collateral, was the first theatrically released digital movie.

533.Celebrities have to pay $30,000 to obtain a star on the Hollywood Walk of Fame.

534.In 2012, an entire village in Sodeto in Spain won the lottery... except one guy. He was very sad.

535.In 2016, a Chinese man tried to sell his daughter for $3,500 so he could buy an iPhone and a motorcycle.

536.A Heisenbug is a computer virus which

changes its behavior if it is observed by the computer user.

537. Golf balls can reach speeds of 170mph when struck with a club.

538. While St. Lawrence was being executed by being held to a red-hot gridiron, he said, "Turn me over, I'm done on this side." He is now the patron saint of comedians.

539. When a dying hospital patient lives longer than doctors expected, they are known as a FTD. This stands for "Failure to Die."

540. The Ten Commandments are 179 words long. The EU regulations on cabbage sales are 26,911 words long.

541. A 2013 BBC study found that 56% of pilots had fallen asleep while flying. 29% had woken to learn that their co-pilot had also fallen asleep.

542. The petals of a sunflower are classified as single-petalled flowers. This means that a sunflower is made of flowers.

543. There are so many types of apple, that if

you ate a different kind of apple every day, it would take almost 20 years to eat every type.

544. Someone on eBay bought a Cheeto for $99,900 because it looked like Harambe the gorilla.

545. Native Americans played lacrosse to prepare for war.

546. There are 500 types of bananas.

547. The Dead Sea is 8.6 times saltier than the ocean.

548. A Liverpudlian got a tattoo on his lower leg that said, "You'll Never Walk Alone." Years later, he received an injury in Afghanistan and had part of his leg amputated. His leg was cut in such a way, that his tattoo now reads, "You'll Never Walk."

549. In 2003, a 67-year-old woman called Dorothy Fletcher suffered a heart attack on a plane. Naturally, someone asked, "Is there a doctor onboard?" Luckily, there were 15 doctors onboard. To be more specific, there

were 15 cardiologists onboard. They used their expertise to save Fletcher and she made a complete recovery.

550. Chris Benoit was a WWE wrestler who murdered his wife and child on June 11th 2007 before taking his own life. The death of Benoit's wife was mentioned on Wikipedia… 14 hours before her body was discovered. Does this mean that someone else was involved in the murder and mentioned it on Wikipedia? Well, that's when this gets even stranger. Benoit's body was found in his home in Georgia. The IP address of the edit was found in Stamford, Connecticut. That's about a thousand miles away. Want to hear the weirdest part of this story? The IP address that was tracked was right around the corner from the WWE (World Wrestling Entertainment) corporate headquarters. Wait, was the WWE involved? No. What happened was a man (whose name is undisclosed) who lived near WWE HQ tended to fabricate stories about celebrities on Wikipedia. He did this so many times, eventually one of his "lies" turned out to be true. When he learned about the investigation, he immediately submitted an apology and confession. The police

confiscated his computer and concluded that what he written on the site was simply a coincidence. Stranger still, some wrestling fans weren't sure if Benoit was actually dead or if this was an overelaborate storyline for WWE. Now you might think, "Surely, the company wouldn't fabricate the death of a significant figure in the wrestling community?" However, there was a plotline where WWE chairman, Vince McMahon, apparently died in a car explosion. And when did McMahon supposedly die? June 24th 2007... the exact same day that Chris Benoit died.

551. A British couple (their identities are anonymous) fell in love when they realized how much they had in common - they had the same birthday, they were born in the same area, and they were both adopted. Only when they got married, did they learn the truth.... they were twins. They filed for an annulment immediately after.

552. In 2008, Sonny Graham killed himself by shooting himself in the throat.
13 years earlier, Sonny had been given a heart transplant. The heart belonged to Tommy Cottle who also committed suicide

by shooting himself in the throat.

553. For the first 22 years of Georgia's history, lawyers were banned from the country for being "a pest and scourge of mankind."

554. Some banks have therapists who help millionaires who can't mentally comprehend how much money they have.

555. When you have adjusted your TV screen, you will have seen the options to change it to a 4:3 and 16:9 ratios. But what is the difference? Well, let's look at all the ratios used for films. 1:1 is used to evoke a sense of the past. 4:3 is the first ratio used for film and is common for period pieces. 16:9 is the most common ratio nowadays. It's very popular for documentaries and quirky comedies. 21:9 is used for intense dramas and films with epic landscapes. The Dark Knight trilogy and The Lord of the Rings trilogy have made this ratio popular.

556. Google Maps calculates traffic by tracking how fast Android devices are moving on the road.

557. Instead of saying, "Not my problem," the

Polish use the expression, "Not my circus, not my monkey."

558. The movie, Cannibal Holocaust, has such realistic death scenes, that the cast had to go to court to prove that the director hadn't killed them.

559. Ice-hockey player, Wayne Gretsky, holds the NHL record for the most goals scored – 2,857. His brother, Brent, has scored four.

560. The most disliked video on YouTube is Justin Bieber's "Baby," with over 4.8 million Dislikes.

561. No numbers from 1-999 contain the letter "a."

562. When Carl Scheele discovered oxygen in 1772, he called it "fire air."

563. Oreos are a rip-off of the Hydrox cookie. Sadly, when Oreos became popular, consumers assumed the Hydrox was a rip-off of Oreos and their company sank into obscurity.

564. Breatharians are people who believe

humanity only needs oxygen to live and don't need food or drink.

565. The residents of Whitesboro, New York, were asked to vote on a town emblem. The choices given were variations of a white man and a Native American holding hands. In the end, the residents decided to maintain their old emblem of a white man choking a Native because it was "friendly."

566. Manute Bol is the tallest basketball player in NBA history, standing 7ft 7. He is also the only player to have killed a lion with a spear.

567. Play-doh was originally called Kutol Rainbow Modelling Compound.

568. A woman lost her wedding ring and found it 16 years later growing on a carrot in her garden.

569. A Japanese soldier was stranded on an island for 30 years, unaware that World War II had ended. His commander had to confront him in 1974 and personally relieve him of his duty.

570. Monopoly has led to several murders after

players became furious that they lost. One murderer killed his friend with an arrow to the chest after he lost the game.

571. The state of Missouri sentenced Mike Anderson to 13 years in jail for armed robbery.

     At the end of the 13 years, law enforcement realized that they had forgotten to put Mike in jail and he had been a free man the whole time.

572. A US college student in 1979 had to work 182 hours per year to pay for tuition. The average 2013 student had to work 991 hours.

573. Every particle of you was created in the heart of a star. But so was garbage so don't get too excited.

574. Neanderthals made toys for their children.

575. The Marx Brothers were a comedy group during the 1930s. They were banned in Ireland for their "anarchic tendencies."

576. If you do not have a gluten allergy, you can become ill by switching to a gluten-free diet.

577. Niccoli Paganini was probably the greatest violinist ever. He was so good, many people believed he was the son of the Devil. He had to publicly reveal letters written to him by his mother to prove that he had a human parent.

578. Different studies have shown that coffee prevents cancer, causes cancer, make you live longer, makes you die prematurely, increases the chances of getting diabetes, and reduces the chances of suffering diabetes.

579. Pacemakers, baby monitors, traffic lights, cars, and even toilets can be hacked.

580. Jon Minnoch was the heaviest man ever weighing at 1,400lbs (100 stone.) He also has the world record for losing the most weight after he shed 924lbs.

581. On March 1st 2017, Antarctica and Cairo were the same temperature – 17.5 degrees Celsius.

582. Beijing is the most polluted city in the world. A video screen of a blue sky was set

up on January 23rd 2013 in Beijing to show
people how the sky should look.

583.Sometimes, surgeons will use coded terms
around patients to avoid scaring them.
When a surgeon says, "bury the hatchet," it
means that instruments have been left
inside a patient.

584.The Deep Web makes up 90% of the
Internet but cannot be accessed through
conventional means.

585.12% of people dream in black-and-white.

586.NASCAR drivers don't need to have a
driver's license to drive in track
competitions.

587.66% of people have never seen snow.

588.In 2012, a group of thieves in Czech
Republic stole an entire bridge.

589.The 44m Midnight Planetarium is a watch
that shows the movements of Mercury,
Venus, Earth, Mars, and Jupiter relative to
the Sun with incredible accuracy. It also tells
the time.

590. The Mekong River in Thailand shoots fireballs every October. Nobody knows why.

591. Pizza Hut has a pizza-flavored perfume.

592. Medieval archers were so strong, they could fire an arrow the distance of three football fields. Archeologists can distinguish an archer in a group of medieval corpses because their bow-arm is abnormally large.

593. The vampire bat is the only bat that can walk. Weirdly, it can walk forwards, sideways, and backwards.

594. Approximately 41% of US citizens believe that people and dinosaurs co-existed.
    They didn't.

595. When a mechanic in the UK noticed the Google Street View car was coming towards him, he staged a murder scene because he thought it would be funny for a homicide to appear on Google Earth. It took a year for police to inquire about the murder.

596. 90% of volcanic eruptions occur

underwater.

597.The hacking group, Anonymous, was created as a joke on 4chan.

598.The most understood term in the world is "OK." The second-most understood is "Coca-Cola."

599.Pope John Paul II was an honorary Globetrotter.

600.When Coca-Cola was originally advertised in China, it was mistranslated as "Bite the wax tadpole." Nowadays, it translates into "to allow the mouth to rejoice."

601.In 1912, Charles Dawson discovered the Missing Link between man and our ancestor. This link (known as the Piltdown Man) was accepted by the scientific community for 40 years before someone noticed that the "link" was a human skull with an orangutan's jaw.

602.Before the hair dryer was perfected, people blow-dried their hair with their vacuum cleaner.

603. The Carpuccino is a car that was fueled by coffee. It could drive 210 miles on a full tank.

604. Laser Tag was created by the US military to train infantry.

605. Lasers can freeze certain materials.

606. Eating mince pies on Christmas day in England used to be illegal. Some sources say that it is still against the law, but it was abolished by Charles II at the end of the 17th century.

607. Netflix was formed because the creators despised the video rental company, Blockbusters.

608. The average Netflix user takes two minutes to choose a movie.

609. According to physicists, the Granny Style is the best way to shoot a ball in basketball. Very few players adopt this technique because it looks silly.

610. The jumping cholla is a cactus that shoots parts of itself at anything that comes near it.

611. The El Diablo Restaurant in the Canary Islands cooks customers' meals over an active volcano.

612. Pineapples used to cost $10,000.

613. A jumbo jet uses 4,000 gallons of fuel to lift off.

614. There are companies that allow you to mix your ashes into fireworks so you can literally "go out with a bang."

615. Go is a board game that was invented in China 2,500 years ago. It is the oldest board game that is still played in its original form.

616. If a character died in a play in Ancient Rome, it was not uncommon to cast a criminal in the part and have them die for real on stage.

617. Since McDonalds has a "doors always open policy" in some countries, homeless people live in the restaurants, especially in Hong Kong and Japan. They are known as McRefugees.

618. A biscuit survived the sinking of the Titanic because it was in the lifeboat survival kit. It was bought at an auction for $23,000 and is known as the "world's most valuable biscuit."

619. 3% of the world's water is drinkable. 0.3% of that drinkable water resides in rivers and lakes.

620. In 1439, King Henry VI of England banned kissing.

621. Sometimes, doctors write "TEETH" on their medical release papers. It's an acronym for "tried everything else, try homeopathy." Basically, it means the doctor has no idea how to treat the patient.

622. Wunderland Kalkar was a nuclear power plant in Germany that was shut down before it was fully constructed. Instead, it was turned into an amusement park.

623. Goldstone Books in south Wales stocked up on tons of copies 50 Shades of Grey, assuming that demand for the #1 Best-Seller would be through the roof. However, almost nobody in the area bought it so the

books were turned into a fort.

624. Summer holidays became official in the 1800s because it was simply too hot for children to go to school.

625. Woo Bum-kon travelled to several villages, shooting people and lobbing grenades into crowds. By the end of his killing spree, he had murdered 56 people and injured 35 others. When he was asked why he killed so many people, he said he was mad because a fly interrupted his sleep that morning with its incessant buzzing.

626. In 1980, Maureen Wilcox picked the correct numbers for the lottery in Massachusetts lottery and the Rhode Island. However, she didn't win any money because she played the winning numbers for each lottery on the other ticket!

627. Adele's full name is Adele Laurie Blue Adkins.

628. Alexander I of Yugoslavia refused to attend public events on Tuesdays because three of his family members died on that day. When he finally agreed to attend a

public event on a Tuesday, he was assassinated.

629. Barbie Soper gave birth to her three children on 08/08/08, 09/09/09 and 10/10/10. The chances of this happening are 50 million to one.

630. The chances of getting struck by lighting is 300,000 to 1. Park ranger, Roy C. Sullivan, has been struck by lightning seven times, which is the world record. The chances of this happening is 1 in 22 septilllion. That's one in a 22,000,000,000,000,000,000,000,000 chance. Although this is quite a famous random fact, there is another interesting thing about Sullivan. He has got into a fight with a bear on 22 separate occasions.

631. In 1990, a 15-year-old student called James Bond sat for his GCSE exam in Argoed High School in Flintshire, Wales. His exam reference number was 007.

632. A man was hit and killed by a truck while he was crossing a highway on his bike, 372 miles north of Helsinki. Two hours later, another man was hit and killed by a truck

while he was crossing a highway on his bike,
372 miles north of Helsinki.
Could this coincidence be any weirder?
They were identical twins.

633. In 1660, a ship sank in Dover. The only
survivor was a man called Hugh Williams. In
1767, another ship sank in the same spot.
The only survivor was a man called Hugh
Williams. In 1820, Hugh Williams was the
lone survivor of a capsized ship on the
Thames. In 1940, a German explosive
destroyed a ship, killing all but two people.
The survivors were both called Hugh
Williams.

634. Dennis Hwang doodled the Google logo.
He is now Google's Chief Doodler.

635. The Netherlands and the Isles of Scilly
fought in the 335 Years War. Nobody died.

636. In 2008, over a million Robbie Williams
CDs were used to build roads in China.

637. "Queue" is the only English word that
sounds the same when you remove the last
four letters.

638. The Eiffel Tower is half a foot taller when it's warm due to thermal expansion.

639. Dolly Parton's husband has seen her perform live once.

640. The mini skirt's name is derived from the Mini Cooper car.

641. The world's oldest operating school is the King's School in Canterbury, England. It was built in 597 AD.

642. A palindrome is a word or phrase that reads the same backwards e.g. "step on no pets," or "A man, a plan, a canal, Panama!" The weirdest palindrome is "Mr owl ate my metal worm" because it is an anagram of itself!

643. A semordnilap is a word or phrase that reads something else if read backwards e.g. "desserts" becomes "stressed" and "repaid" becomes "diaper." "Semordnilap" is a palindrome since it spells "palindrome" backwards.

644. In The Hobbit movies, Smaug the dragon has 2,690 tons of gold. By comparison, the

US's reserve contains 8,134 tons of gold.

645. Water is the most consumed drink in the world. The second-most common is tea.

646. Tea was discovered in 2737 BC.

647. In Ancient Egypt, couples were considered married if they lived together.

648. The average person spends less than one minute on an Internet page before clicking on something else.

649. The Olympics stopped firing a pistol before races because it took too long for the sound to carry over to athletes who were furthest away.

650. In Luxembourg, secondary students must be trilingual to graduate. Most students learn French, German and Luxembourgish.

651. Polls have shown that lab technicians drink more coffee than people in any other profession.

652. There was a Bible shortage in 1943 due to WWII.

653. There are websites that allow you to hire a person who will queue on your behalf. Line-sitters can make up to $1,000 per week.

654. New parents lose about 750 hours of sleep per year when they have a baby.

655. If you want to win a hand-drawn raffle, wrinkle your entry. It will take up more space and feel different from the others, making it stand out.

656. Tug of War used to be an Olympic sport.

657. iTunes used to have an app called I Am Rich that cost $999. Although it served no purpose, eight people bought it before it was removed from the app store.

658. You can hire a professional lice remover in the US. Although this sounds like a stupid job, it is quite important because American students with lice are sent home from school and are not allowed to go back unless they can prove the lice have gone.

659. It takes five years of training to become a professional tea taster.

660. The cereal mascot, Cap'n Crunch's, real name is Horatio Magellan.

661. A company in New York introduced pencils to schools that read, "Too cool to do drugs" on the side. They had to be recalled when the company realized that as the pencils were sharpened, the message read, "Do drugs."

662. "Bookkeeper" is the only English word that has three consecutive double letters.

663. The Eiffel Tower has 1,665 steps.

664. The Monopoly mascot is called Rich Uncle Pennybags. The police officer on the Go Directly To Jail spot is called Officer Edgar Mallory. The man in the In Jail spot is called Jake the Jailbird.

665. Barbie's full name is Barbara Millicent Roberts. Her partner is called Ken Carson.

666. Ruth Handler created the Barbie doll. Her daughter never owned a Barbie.

667. When someone says, "Think of a card" the

most likely card that people think of is the Ace of Spades, then the Queen of Hearts and then the King of Hearts.

The least likely card to be chosen are the 7 of Spades, 5 of Clubs, the 6 of Clubs, and the 5 of Diamonds.

668. 40% of schizophrenics are left-handed.

669. Casper the Friendly Ghost's surname is McFadden.

670. The patient in the board game, Operation, is called Cavity Sam.

671. In 2015, the national debt of the US was $14,433,723,192,124. That means each US citizen owes $122,303.

672. The Michelin Man's real name is Bibendum.

673. In the 1800s, people bought mummies and had Mummy Unwrapping Parties.

674. "Eleven plus two" is an anagram of "twelve plus one."

675. In Japan, you can pay a professional

cuddler $80 per hour to hug you.

676. In 2014, a man sued McDonalds for $1.5 million because he only received one napkin with his food, which forced him to suffer "undue mental anguish."

677. The electric chair was invented by a dentist.

678. An arctophile is a person who is obsessed with teddy bears.

679. In 2009, a man tried to sue his ex-wife for custody of the kidney he had donated to her. His claim was rejected.

680. In 1989, Disney forced three daycare centers to remove pictures of Mickey Mouse, Minnie, and Goofy that were painted on the walls because the paintings breached Disney's copyright.

681. Richard Branson drinks 20 cups of tea every day.

682. Young children, especially twins, often develop their own language that is unintelligible to everyone except them.

683. The original purpose for groomsmen was to protect the bride by preventing her from being captured during the wedding.

684. The oldest word in the English language is "town."

685. There is no leap year every 400 years.

686. After the Kids Wish Network raised $127 million, researchers wanted to see how much of the money went to children in need.
$109.8 million went to telemarketers.
$18.1 million went to charity workers.
$3.2 million went to dying children.

687. Gabriel Garcia Moreno was the president of Ecuador in the 19th century. As he was leaving a cathedral one day, he was attacked by assassins with machetes. Although his neck, skull, and brain were sliced through, and he had his arm lopped off, he remained standing. He was slashed 14 times and shot six times before he fell to the ground. He wrote, "God does not die" in his own blood moments before he died.

688. Although Oprah is famous for giving out

free cars, many people don't know that the audience members who receive this gift have to pay $7,000 in taxes or forfeit the gift.

689. You cannot dream and snore simultaneously.

690. In 2006, renowned magician, David Copperfield, used sleight of hand to convince armed robbers that he had nothing in his pockets, when in fact he was carrying his passport, wallet and cellphone.

691. Former boxer, George Foreman, named five of his children George Foreman.

692. Mickey Mouse is the first non-human to win an Oscar.

693. There's a monument in Russia of a laboratory mouse knitting a piece of DNA. It represents all the mice who have died in scientific experiments for the benefit of humanity.

694. If a Caribbean spiny lobster learns that a neighboring lobster is ill, the spiny lobster will shun it.

695.   Many French citizens in Landes had to wear stilts during the 19th century because the swamps in the region were so muddy.

696.   The Story of Ferdinand is about a bull which prefers to smell flowers rather than fight matadors. During World War II, it was banned in Italy, Germany and Russia for being "too nice."

697.Apes suffer from mid-life crises.

698.Blue makes you appear more trustworthy, conservative, and secure. Red makes you appear powerful, energetic, and inspirational. Politicians and presidents usually wear red ties, especially during difficult times.

699.If you type "elgoog" into a Google search engine, it will send you to a backwards version of the site.

700.Dolly Parton entered a Dolly Parton look-a-like contest and lost. Adele also lost an Adele look-a-like contest and lost.

701.316 entries in Webster's 1996 dictionary

were misspelt.

702. When news host, Mika Brzezinksi, was expected to read a story about Paris Hilton, she placed her papers in the shredder because she was sick and tired of being given gossipy non-news stories. She has become a hero to many feminists.

703. Seven million tons of garbage is dumped into the ocean every year. Most of it is plastic.

704. Spending a day in Mumbai in India carries the same health risks as smoking 100 cigarettes a day.

705. "Facetious," "abstcmious," and "arsenious" contain all the vowels in the correct order.

706. Climbing Mt. Everest cost at least $60,000 but it can cost up to $120,000.

707. James Lewis was adopted as a baby, having been separated from his twin brother at birth. When he grew up he married a woman called Linda, divorced her, then married a woman called Betty who

had a son called James Alan.

Years later, he tracked down his twin brother, James Springer. Springer had also married a woman called Linda, divorced her, married another woman called Betty and had a son called James Alan.

708. From 1977 to 1979, the Montreal Juniors hockey team had three players called Denis Savard, Denis Tremblay, and Denis Cyr. By a complete coincidence, they all grew up on the same street.

In a bizarre twist of fate, they were all born on February 4th 1961.

709. Two women went into an office to register a complaint since they had been allotted the same social security number. They learned that they were both called Patricia Ann Campbell and were born on March 13th 1941. Their fathers were called Robert and they had both married military men in 1959 and had two children that were aged 21 and 19.

710. A man called Armand Hammer coincidentally became a member of the board of directors for Arm & Hammer.

711. There are 100 divorces every hour in the US.

712. Most antibiotics are made from bacteria.

713. The Bajau people are the only people on Earth that don't live on land. They have built houses on water and claim to have no nationality.

714. 50 million people in the world are drunk at any one time.

715. Daniel "Rubberboy" Browning Smith is the most flexible person in the world. His stretching ability has enabled him to hold five Guinness World Records. He can turn his torso 180 degrees and can fit his entire body through a tennis racquet.

716. A man tried to sue David Blaine for $50 million for supposedly stealing his magical powers.

717. Major league Baseball umpires must wear black underwear.

718. It is legal to kill a Scotsman with a bow and arrow if he enters the city of York in the

UK. However, this law is not enforced. It would be weird if it was.

719. Approximately one hundred Russians die every year from falling ice.

720. The Sanskrit language has 96 words for "love."

721. 66% of all US cash is held overseas.

722. Originally, the dolls, Barbie and Ken, were brother and sister.

723. In Ancient Greece, people showed affection by throwing apples at one another.

724. Men are five times more likely to be struck by lightning than women.

725. Starbucks spends more money on its employees' health insurance than on coffee beans.

726. The last scoreless NFL game was in 1943.

727. Bananas are curved because they grow towards the sun.

728. McDonalds Golden Arches are more recognizable worldwide than the Christian cross.

729. Evan Booth wanted to demonstrate the flaws in airport security by showing that he could turn items available at the airport gift shop into weapons. He turned dental floss, copies of US Weekly, and souvenir magnets into a nunchaku. He turned a hair dryer, an umbrella, and braided rope into a crossbow. He turned a hair dryer, a hair band, 9x9v batteries, a fridge magnet clip, magazines, tape, dental floss, aluminum, and a can of Red Bull into a gun.

730. When a tennis player grunts while hitting the ball, it increases the ball's velocity by 4%.

731. You are more likely to earn a position in Harvard university than get a position at Apple.

732. 6% of American adults can't ride a bike.

733. Marital infidelity was punishable with jail time in South Korea until 2015.

734. Being a waterslide critic is a real job. It's surprisingly well-paid.

735. People in the Western world usually say "Cheese" when they are having their picture taken. Chinese people say the Chinese word for eggplant when they are having their picture taken.

736. The Ancient Greek philosopher, Chrysippus, died after laughing too hard at a joke. It was a joke he told.

737. In 2011, the US Congress declared that pizza and French fries could be classified as vegetables for school lunch dinners.

738. Submarine cables run thousands of miles under the ocean to connect each country to the Internet.

739. Rhubarb leaves can be poisonous.

740. In 1984, Janet Harris broke a world record by eating 7,175 peas in one hour using chopsticks.

741. -40 degrees Celsius and -40 degrees Fahrenheit are the same temperature.

742. Barbie was co-designed by a missile designer.

743. Kurt Godel was terrified of being poisoned and only ate food that was prepared by his wife. When she was hospitalized for six months, he refused to eat and died, weighing just 65lbs.

744. Frederick William I was the king of Prussia during the 18th century. He was so obsessed with tall people that all his soldiers had to be at least 6ft tall. He bought tall children from their parents, kidnapped tall men, and forced them to marry tall women. Sometimes, he stretched people on a rack to make them taller.

745. The city of Johannesburg has been completely rebuilt four times.

746. A cricket game between England and South Africa went on for 14 days.

747. If you took all the molecules in a teaspoon of water and lined them up, it would stretch out for 30 billion miles. That's 322 times the distance between the Earth and the Sun.

748.iPhone factories produce 36,000 phones in 12 hours.

749.Iran has the highest female to male ratio in universities among all sovereign nations. Over 70% of students in subjects such as engineering and science are female.

750.According to researchers in China, most people who win Rock-Paper-Scissors will choose the same action that made them win the previous game. This study showed that if you lost the last round, you should choose the action that would have beaten the winner in that round. If you won the last round, you should choose one of the actions that the loser did not use in the previous game.

751.Honeycombs, dragonfly wings, dried-up soil, and tomato skins all have a hexagonal structure.

752.The first man to survive going over Niagara Falls died by slipping on an orange peel.

753.66% of US citizens believe in love at first

sight.

754. In 2014, a 62-year-old man tried to sue several corporations for two undecillion dollars. First off, that's a real number. It looks like this – 2,000,000,000,000,000,000,000,000,000,000,000,000. Secondly, that's 246,913,580,000,000,000,000,000 times more money than exists on Earth.

755. Each Google container holds 1,160 servers. Each warehouse contains 200,000 servers. Google must shift around 1-2 million servers every time you check something on their site.

756. A man called Jack Ass tried to sue the show, Jackass, for plagiarizing his name and defaming him.

757. It takes two years for a pineapple to mature.

758. Until 1000 AD, coffee beans were eaten, not brewed.

759. The first popular version of Photoshopping dates back to 1856. During

the Victorian era, portraits of people without their heads were quite common.

760.The Russian armed forces offer women sniper duties as they believe that females are more careful, patient and nimble than men.

761.When Hollywood actress, Jodie Foster, was 10, she was attacked by a lion and carried in its mouth.

762.There is the equivalent of 22 packs of sugar in 200oz of Coca Cola.

763.Five billion copies of the Bible have been sold.

764.250 children at the University of Sheffield were polled to see how many liked clowns. The result was zero.

765.In Spanish, the word "esposas" means both "wives" and "handcuffs."

766.Google was nearly called Backrub.

767.According to a study performed by the Michigan State University, only 5% of US citizens wash their hands after they use the toilet.

768. Kiwis used to be called Chinese gooseberries.

769. A speck of dust is halfway between the size of an atom and the Earth.

770. 90% of US citizens can't name the four presidents that appear on Mt. Rushmore.

771. One of the soldiers who served in WWI was eight years old.

772. If a helicopter tilts its tail too high, the tail will be chopped off by the own propeller.

773. During the Carboniferous period (359-299 million years ago,) trees didn't decompose.

774. The Berlandiera lyrata flower smells like chocolate.

775. You can change your language on Facebook to "Pirate."

776. There's only a 10% chance a lightning strike will kill you.

777. Drinking a quart of soy sauce in one gulp can leave you in a coma.

778. When the nuclear bomb hit Hiroshima at 8:15am on August 6th 1945, 100,000 people died in 43 seconds.

779. If you shouted for eight years, seven months, and six days, you would produce enough sound energy to heat one cup of coffee.

780. 15% of US citizens believe the world will end in their lifetime.

781. 10% of US citizens thought the world would end in 2012.

782. At least 12 people have died while karaoke singing Frank Sinatra's My Way in the Philippines between 2002-2012. This coincidence is so bizarre, that My Way Killings has its own page on Wikipedia.

783. On July 28th 1900, King Umberto I of Italy ate at a restaurant in Monza. He learned he shared many similarities with the owner of the restaurant.

i)   They had the same birthday.
ii)   They were born in the town of Turin.
iii)   They both married women called
        Margherita on the same day.
iv)   The restaurant opened the day Umberto
        became king.
v)   They were both called Umberto.
The day after this encounter, the king
learned that the restaurant owner had been
shot dead. Minutes later, the king was
assassinated.

784.   A carpenter called Michael Dick traveled
throughout England searching for his long-lost daughter, Lisa. A local paper took a recent photograph of Michael with his two other daughters for an article. When Lisa was reunited with her father, she realized that she was behind Michael when the local paper took his photograph.

785. Ramon Artagaveytia's ship sunk in 1871, which left him with a severe phobia of sailing. In 1912, after over 40 years, he finally decided to sail again. He died when the ship, the Titanic, sank.

786. Soy sauce contains 10 times more antioxidants than red wine.

787. Toothpaste looks like a purple crystal in its purest form.

788. A lot of candles and soap in France during the 18th century were made from human bodies.

789. The great auk was a bird that went extinct in the 1840s. The last auk was killed after it was mistaken for a witch.

790. 44,000 years ago, rats were ten times bigger than they are today.

791. The Mycocepurus smithii ant can clone itself. When a female ant learned how to duplicate itself, all the male ants were kicked out of the colony and eventually died out. The all-female colony is now self-sustaining.

792. In 1386, a pig in France was executed by public hanging for murdering a child.

793. The Bible exists in 2,454 languages.

794. The first record of a ninja was a 13-year-old Japanese boy called Hino Kumawaka.

795. Tickling was used as a form of torture in Ancient China.

796. Flushing a toilet sends bacteria up to two meters around your bathroom.

797. You need to walk the full length of a football field to burn off one M&M.

798. The average British person has 396 friends over his or her lifetime.

799. In 2014, a group of researchers concluded that the catchiest song ever was Wannabe by The Spice Girls. Listeners could recognize the song within 2.3 seconds. The average length of time it takes to recognize a song is five seconds. The second-catchiest song was Lou Bega's Mambo #5. The third-catchiest song was the Rocky IV theme song, Eye of the Tiger.

800. While walking, you can increase your metabolic rate by 12% by not swinging your arms.

801. You need to have at least 51% of a US bill intact for it to be considered legal currency.

802. The average household with two
teenagers has 10 devices that can connect to
the Internet.

803. 90% of the world's population lives in the
Northern Hemisphere.

804. If your car could drive upward at 60mph,
it would take an hour to reach outer space
and six months to reach the Moon.

805. Seven million smartphones are dropped
down the toilet per year.

806. Westerners consume approximately 50
tons of food and 50,000 liters of liquid in
their lifetime.

807. Marjorie Gestring won an Olympic gold
medal for diving in 1936. She was only 13 at
the time, making her the youngest person to
win an Olympic gold medal.

808. Eddie "the Eagle" Edwards was a British
man who came last in two Olympic ski-
jumps. In his later life, he released a song in
Finnish, even though he doesn't speak the
language.

809. The reason people like crispy foods such as crisps and pretzels is because when our ancestors used to eat insects and plants, the most telling way to know if the food was fresh was from its crispiness. Our brains are naturally hardwired to think crispy food is healthy.

810. If you talk to somebody that you like while you walk, your footsteps will instinctively synchronize with theirs'.

811. The Ivanpah Solar Electric Generating System in California's Mojave Desert has over 300,000 computer-controlled mirrors which track the Sun and cover 3,500 acres of land. They provide power for over 140,000 houses.

812. The longest wedding dress had a train that was 1.85 miles long.

813. The lighter was invented before the match.

814. It's common knowledge that wide skirts became popular in the mid-19th century. Many wearers assumed that the bigger their

skirt, the more fashionable they would come across. This became a problem as some women would wear skirts that were so big, they couldn't fit through doorways.

815. The shortest time elapsed before a red card was given in a game of football was two seconds. It was give to Lee Todd after he complained the whistle was too loud.

816. The average person spends three years on the toilet throughout their life.

817. 18% of Americans believe they have seen a ghost.

818. If you drew one line with an average lead pencil, it would go on for 35 miles.

819. Before gay marriage was legal in the US, Foxnews.com showed a photo of a married male and female to promote "traditional marriage." However, they didn't realize that the couple in the photo were two women, Lela McArthur and Stephanie Figarelle.

820. If you tell Paul Erdos how old you are, he can calculate how many seconds you have lived. He can make this calculation in three

seconds. He has been able to do this since he was four.

821. Under a microscope, Velcro looks like lava with tentacles.

822. If a battery bounces, it's empty. If a battery hits the ground and then falls over, it's full.

823. Farthings and shillings are often mentioned in old English dramas but few people outside of Britain know how much these coins are worth. Four farthings equaled a penny. 12 pennies equaled a shilling. 20 shillings equaled a pound.

824. China has treatment camps for Internet addicts.

825. The destruction of the Twin Towers destroyed a lot more than two buildings. Three other center buildings collapsed as well as a church. Four other buildings were damaged beyond repair and had to be destroyed. Dozens more buildings took years to fix.

826. Tong Aonan solved 840 Rubik's cubes and formed them together to create a picture of

a girl he had a crush on. He used it to declare his love for her. She turned him down.

827. 8% of people accomplish their New Year's Resolution.

828. The Dracula Simia flower looks like it has a monkey face.

829. The Orchis Italica flower looks like two naked men holding hands.

830. The Anguloa Uniflora flower looks like a baby inside a crib.

831. The Impatiens Psittacina flower looks like a parrot.

832. The Aristolochia Salvadorensis flower looks like Darth Vader's helmet.

833. The Caleana Major flower looks like a duck that's about to take flight.

834. The Habenaria Grandifloriformis flower looks like an angel.

835. The Antirrhinum plant looks like a human

skull.

836. The Impatiens Bequaertii flower looks like a dancing baby with a pacifier in its mouth.

837. The Psychotria Elata flower looks like a pair of woman's lips about to kiss someone.

838. Black cars get involved in more crashes than cars of any other color.

839. A woman took part in a search for a missing tourist in Iceland. Hours later, she learned that she was the supposed missing person.

840. 5,000 people die daily from unclean water.

841. In 88 years, only one woman has ever won an Oscar for Best Director.

842. No black person has ever won an Oscar for Best Director.

843. For every thousand films directed, only 45 of them are made by women.

844. It has become so unbearably hot in Vietnam in recent summers, that people

have started wearing random objects like cardboard boxes and plant pots to block out the Sun.

845. The 1896 film, The Haunted Castle, was the first horror film ever made.

846. 925 million people will eat nothing today.

847. There are more US politicians in the world than pandas.

848. There are approximately 3,000 types of microbes that can be found on paper money.

849. Pirates used to think that gold earrings improved their sight.

850. The cleanest continent on Earth is Antarctica. It also has the highest education.

851. Vikings usually gave kittens to their new brides.

852. 30,000 websites are hacked every day.

853. The film, Titanic, cost $200 million to make. The actual Titanic took $7 million to build.

854. There are more people in Tokyo than in Canada, even though Canada is the second largest country on Earth.

855. The Oscar panel can choose what film they want to win Best Picture even if they haven't seen all the nominated films. In fact, this happens almost every year.

856. After multiple students were shot dead at Columbine high school, Marilyn Manson was asked what he would say to the shooters. Manson answered, "I wouldn't say a single word to them. I would listen to what they have to say, and that's what no one did."

857. A homeless man in Portland robbed a bank for $1, then sat down and waited for the police to arrest him so he could receive healthcare in prison.

858. The "Million Dollar Paranormal challenge" was created by James Randi. He has offered $1 million to anyone who can prove they are psychic. In 40 years, no one has ever beaten his challenge.

859. Since scientists have found so many brain-

controlling parasites, they believe that a human zombie apocalypse is possible.

860.A tomato has 7,000 more genes than a human.

861.Sunflowers absorb radioactive waste.

862."Candidate" used to mean "white toga."

863.In Ancient Rome, soldiers had slaves who whispered "You are just a man" to stop the warriors from getting cocky in battle.

864.Anechoic chambers at the Technical University of Denmark are designed to absorb the echo of radio, sound, and microwaves. These chambers are said to be the quietest rooms in the world. They are so quiet, that if you were inside them, you would hear your own organs churning around your body. Many people can't stay in the room for too long as it makes them feel uncomfortable.

865.A 9,000-year-old skeleton was discovered in a cave in Cheddar, England. The body is now known as the Cheddar Man. When his DNA was tested, the researchers learned that he had a descendant who worked as a teacher only half a mile away. The Cheddar Man and the teacher are linked 300 generations apart.

866. Norman Mailer wrote about a Russian spy in his novel, Barbary Shore. After the novel was published, the US Immigration Service arrested a Russian spy who happened to live one floor above Mailer. He was Colonel Rudolf Abel, who happened to be the most efficient Russian spy in the US at the time.

867. Legendary actor, James Dean, met Oscar-winner, Alec Guinness, while he was shooting a film called The Swan. When Guinness saw Dean's Porsche, he said, "Get rid of that car, or you'll be dead in a week!" Dean died in a car crash several days later. Although this coincidence is quite well-known, it gets stranger.

i)   When Dean's car was towed away, its engine fell out and crushed the mechanic's legs.

ii)   The engine was bought by a doctor for his race car. He died shortly after during a race. Another racer in the same race was killed. His car had Dean's driveshaft fitted to it.

iii)   When Dean's Porsche was repaired, the garage it resided in burned down.

iv)   When the Porsche was displayed in Sacramento, the platform it was on collapsed and the car hit into a teenager, breaking his hip.

v)   In Oregon, the car's trailer slipped from its towbar and smashed through a shop.

vi)   In 1959, the car finally put itself out of its misery when it mysteriously shattered into 11 pieces while it was sitting on steel supports.

868. When Joseph Aigner was 18 years old, he tried to hang himself. Thankfully, he was saved by a mysterious Capuchin monk. When he was 22, he tried to hang himself again but was stopped by the very same monk. Eight years later, he was sentenced to death for treason. Luckily, he was acquitted when he was defended...by the same monk. When Aigner was 68, he finally succeeded in taking his own life, shooting himself in the head. His eulogy was performed by the very same Capuchin monk. This monk kept encountering Aigner for half a century and yet, Aigner never learned his name.

869. John Parr was the first British soldier to

die in action during the World War I. The last British soldier to die was George Ellison. By a complete coincidence, their graves face each other at St Symphorian cemetery near Mons.

870. Belgium used to have chocolate stamps.

871. The biggest land vehicle in the world is the 228 Bucket-Wheel Excavator in Germany. It can excavate 240,000 tons of coal per day.

872. There is a garbage pile in the Pacific Ocean that is the size of Texas.

873. A Chicago high school set up a fundraiser by playing Justin Bieber music and the students had to pay to stop it. They raised $1,000 in three days.

874. A ball of glass will bounce higher than a ball of rubber.

875. Humans and bananas share 50% of the same genes.

876. There is a tree that sprouts seven completely different fruits. It is called the

Fruit Salad tree.

877. The pagoda temple in Horyuji, Japan, is the world's oldest wooden building. Some of the timber came from trees felled around 600 AD.

878. A Swedish couple named their kid Brfxxccxxmnpcccclllmmnprxvclmnckssqlbb 111116. His name is pronounced "Albin."

879. In 2009, a teenager impersonated a cop in the Chicago Police Department. He worked a full shift, drove a squad car, and arrested someone.

880. In Ancient Roman times, crocodile meat was used to get rid of freckles. It didn't work.

881. Ketchup becomes thinner when shaken. Nobody knows why.

882. There was a time where every British male older than six had to wear a hat on Sunday.

883. The world's largest chocolate bar weighed 12,770lbs.

884.   Territorio de Zaguates is an enormous
       sanctuary in Costa Rica that holds over
       1,000 stray dogs.

885. In 1985, a bear ate 75lbs of cocaine and
     then died of an overdose. He is known as
     Pablo EskoBear.

886. In early 2016, coyotes were spotted on
     Highway 1 near Bolinas in California. At
     first, no one knew why the coyotes were
     wandering onto the dangerous road. Then
     the truth came out – they were high. The
     coyotes were disoriented and wandering
     around because they were eating fly agaric
     mushrooms that were growing nearby.
     These types of fungi are intensely
     hallucinogenic.

887. Only a licensed electrician is legally
     allowed to change a lightbulb in Victoria,
     Australia.

888. Edward Palmer invented the stocks in
     Boston. The stocks were a wooden device
     that locked criminals in a seated or standing
     position and people then threw rotten
     vegetables at them. And who was the first

person to ever be put in the stocks? Edward Palmer. His crime? Charging too much for building stocks.

889.Painite is the rarest crystal in the world. Since the 1950s, only 25 crystals have ever been found. It's so rare that it costs $300,000 per gram.

890.Per mile, you are 27 times more likely to die on a motorcycle than in a car.

891.By the time a First World Country child is eight years old, he or she will have consumed more sugar than an average person did in their entire life a century ago.

892.A Roman emperor called Heliogabalus got party guests so drunk that they passed out. He then left them in a room with toothless leopards, lions, and bears.

893.A passenger at Heathrow was forced to change his T-shirt before being allowed to board a flight because the character on it, Optimus Prime from the Transformer series, was holding a gun.

894.The first speeding ticket was issued in

1896 to Walter Arnold who was driving 8mph. It's a miracle nobody was killed.

895. The wingspan of a Boeing 747 is longer than the entire distance of the Wright Brothers' first flight.

896. Thomas J. Grasso was found guilty of two counts of murder and was executed by lethal injection in 1995. The last thing he ever said was, "Please tell the media I did not get my SpaghettiOs, I got spaghetti. I want the press to know this."

897. During the 18th century, English estate owners hired people to grow their hair and nails and not wash themselves. They then lived in the estate owners' gardens as ornamental hermits.

898. Aitabdel Salem served five months in Rikers Island prison because nobody told him that his bail was $2.

899. John Scurlock invented air cushions that catch people who fall out of burning buildings. Scurlock tweaked the air cushion until it became another invention – the bouncy castle.

900. Dave Archer is a painter. But he doesn't create portraits with paint. Instead, he uses an electric circuit called a Tesla coil. The coil discharges electricity onto Archer's canvas, which he directs to make his picture.

Only word can describe this – Shocking.

901. Japanese Buddhists practice self-mummification. This means they mummify themselves while they are still alive. The process is supposed to take 3,000 days. That's nearly nine years.

902. Chi-chi is London's most famous panda. Originally, she was meant to be transported to the US, but was rejected since she was "communist goods."

903. The cars that are stolen the least are pink, bright yellow, and purple. This is because thieves don't want to stand out after they have stolen a car. Also, nobody wants to drive a yellow car.

904. Omkari Panwar was 72 when she gave birth, making her the oldest mother ever. Just to show off, she had twins.

905.Japan only has a military for defense. By law, they are prohibited from taking part in any missions outside of Japan.

906.The bark of a redwood tree is fireproof. However, these trees can still burn from the inside.

907.In the 1630s, a single tulip in Holland was worth the equivalent of $1,250 in today's money.

908.Elizabeth Blackwell was the first American woman to go to medical school. She was admitted to Geneva Medical School as a joke.

909.The Mars bars company used to own Uncle Ben's rice.

910.Mayra Rosales was found guilty of murdering her nephew in 2008. However, she couldn't go to jail because she weighed 1,036lbs and hadn't left her bedroom for five years. She was the heaviest woman in the world and was known as the Half-Ton Killer. It was eventually revealed that Rosales' sister was the murderer and she was jailed for 15 years. Rosales has since lost 882 lbs.

911. The oldest recorded text is called
Instructions of Shuruppak. This 4,500-year-
old text reads, "Do not pass judgement when
you drink beer."

912. Mikhail Gorbachev is mainly known for
being the leader of the Soviet Union until it
dissolved in 1991. However, few people
know that Gorbachev is also a Grammy
winner.

913. The mascot of McDonalds, Ronald
McDonald, is a clown. Originally, he was
going to be a cowboy.

914. The Breakup Shop is a website that will
dump your partner on your behalf for $10.

915. Approximately 258 babies are born every
minute.

916. You can get the bends in a swimming pool.

917. The Indonesian volcano, Mount Tambora,
erupted in 1816. The eruption was so
intense, it altered the climate so it was
incredibly cold throughout the year. 1816 is

known as The Year Without A Summer.

918. There have been five attempts in history… at banning history.

919. Lava can be as hot as 1,204 degrees Celsius.

920. 21.84% of all published books are in English.

921. When shopping carts were invented, men refused to use them because they were considered "unmanly." The inventor had to hire people to use them in shops before customers gave them a chance.

922. Coke bottles were designed so they could be recognized when they were felt in the dark.

923. The average depth of the ocean is 2.3 miles.

924. The first person in history whose name we know of was a man called Kushim. He was a Mesopotamian accountant who lived around 3200 BC.

925. Harold Hackett has sent 8,000 messages in

bottles. He has received a reply to over half of them.

926. Volcano surfing is a sport. Surfers ride wooden toboggans on the surface of a volcano.

927. Botox was invented to stop muscle spasms in a person's eyelids or vocal chords.

928. Lipstick was a sign of social status in the Roman Republic.

929. There is a skydiver who did 640 jumps in 24 hours.

930. The US army uses robots to remove explosives, mines, weapons, etc. to ensure the safety of the soldiers. However, people grow so attached to the robots that there have been several incidents where soldiers have risked their lives to protect them.

931. Tupac was a ballet dancer.

932. When umbrellas were invented, British people dismissed them because they were "too French-like." When Jonas Hanway used an umbrella in London in the 1750s, people

threw trash at him.

933. Some skydivers throw their parachute out
of the plane and then jumped out and try to
catch it before they hit the ground. This is
called banzai skydiving.

934. The inventor of the Waffle Iron didn't like
waffles.

935. The Cap'N Crunch cereal mascot's real
name is Horatio Magellan.

936. A man tried to blow up the Eiffel Tower
because its light kept him up at night.

937. In Montreal, you can rent a dwarf for
bachelor parties.

938. Only one plane was allowed to take off
after flights were grounded on September
11th 2001. The plane was carrying anti-
venom for a man who was bitten by a snake.

939. The students at Christ's Hospital Boarding
School in England have been wearing the
same uniform since 1556.

940. London has an annual Boring Conference

that discusses monotonous things like sneezing, toast, font types, and the sounds that vending machines make.

941. 3.7 billion years ago, water was green and the sky was orange.

942. Pack Up + Go is a travel company that book flights and hotels for you but don't tell you where you are going. They take your budget into account and then organize three-day weekends to a secret destination.

943. Robert Cornelius was the first person to have his photograph taken facing the camera.

944. A group of vervet monkeys were given alcohol to see how they reacted to it. 5% of the monkeys became binge drinkers.

945. Animals didn't evolve with legs to walk on land. On the contrary, they evolved legs to walk underwater. One of the few animals in modern times that still does this is the anglerfish.

946. Haggis is illegal in the United States.

947.There are beaches in Hawaii with green sand.

948.Priscillian was a priest in Ancient Rome who claimed to be a god-like messiah. The Empire had him beheaded for heresy. This is the first record of a person being beheaded as a government sanctioned punishment. It is also the first time a government and church accused someone of heresy.

949.Any time you see whipped cream in commercials, it's usually shaving cream. This is because whipped cream melts too quickly.

950.The Swedish band, ABBA, were known for wearing ridiculous outfits. However, these silly costumes were actually a strategy to save money on taxes. According to a law in Sweden, the band's wardrobe could only receive a tax deduction if their clothes were "so outrageous that they couldn't be worn on the street."

951."Mother-in-law" is an anagram of "woman Hitler."

952.As a child, Angelina Jolie wanted to be a

funeral director.

953. Sound waves can be used to make objects levitate.

954. An astronaut's suit takes about 5,000 hours to make.

955. Many Japanese people wear kimonos. "Kimono" means "the thing worn."

956. Coffee was banned in Mecca during the 16th century as it was believed the drink made people become "too political."

957. The 50 tallest mountains are all in Asia.

958. Oranges were originally green. When they were this color, they were called geoluread.

959. In 10 minutes, a hurricane releases more energy than all the world's nuclear weapons combined.

960. In 2016, a Bornean orangutan called Kondor did not get on with another orangutan called Sidony. One day, Kondor called another orangutan, Ekko over to her. This was strange as apes of opposite

genders rarely interact outside of mating season. That same day, Ekko was seen watching Sidony and then returning to Kondor. In the end, Ekko mauled Sidony to death. Researchers believe this was the first time in the animal kingdom where a creature "hired an assassin" to take out a target.

961.   Camels were originally adapted to the arctic.

962.   Humans started wearing clothes about 80,000 years ago.

963.   In Japan, the Hiroshima Peace Flame has been burning since 1964. It will continue to burn until all nuclear bombs on the planet are destroyed, freeing the world from the threat of nuclear destruction.

964.   If a horse wins a race "hands down," it means the jockey didn't use his whip.

965.716 million years ago, the Earth was so cold, it looked like a giant snowball if it was observed from space.

966.The longest kiss was 58 hours, 35 minutes

and 58 seconds.

967.Johnny Depp wears blue-tinted glasses because his vision is so bad. He has been nearly completely blind in his left eye since birth.

968.In one episode of The Simpsons, an Australian calls a dollar a "Dollarydoo." Ever since this episode aired, there is an Australian Movement trying to change the name of the Australian Dollar to Dollarydoo.

969.In the James Bond series, Bond has a license to kill. This wasn't made up for the movies. A license to kill does exist. Its official name is a Class Seven authorization.

970.There have been four attempts in British history to ban football.

971.The guillotine was invented to execute criminals quickly and painlessly. However, the blade sometimes jammed and it could take up to 15 minutes for the prisoner to die.

972.Sunspring is a nine-minute short that was released in 2016. It is the first film written by artificial intelligence.

973. During the 18th and 19th century, you
could hire a sin-eater in England. During a
funeral, a loaf of bread was placed on the
recently deceased's chest. The bread was
supposed to absorb all the sins of the dead.
The sin-eater then ate the bread to ensure
the departed went to heaven immediately.

974. There is a conspiracy theory that the
Titanic never sank. The theory suggests that
JP Morgan (who financed the company that
built the Titanic) pretended the ship sank to
claim the insurance money.

975. Every single restaurant that Gordon
Ramsay visited in Season 2 of the US version
of Kitchen Nightmares has closed.

976. The pharmaceutical drugs industry made
$446 billion in the US in 2016.

977. You can tell when a loaf of bread was
baked by the color of its twist tie.
i)   Monday - Blue
ii) Tuesday - Green
iii) Thursday - Red
iv) Friday -White

v) Saturday - Yellow

978. 78% of former NFL players are broke two
     years after retirement.

979. The word "obsession" is derived from the
     word "possession."

980. A woman from New Zealand got arrested
     while she was in Pakistan because they
     didn't believe her country was real.

981.   An Australian Funnel-Web spider has
     fangs strong enough to pierce fingernails
     and shoes.

982.   If you eat fish once per week, it will
     make your brain stronger, thicker. and more
     resilient.

983.   If you ever worry that you can't keep up
     with the younger generation, you're not
     alone. Monkeys have the same problem.
     When younger monkeys introduce new
     customs and habits in their group, it's not
     uncommon for the older monkeys to grow
     frustrated because they can't adjust and so
     they leave.

984.   Primates and marsupials are the only mammals that possess trichromatic vision. This means that these species can see colors that are produced at short, medium and long wavelengths of the light spectrum.

985.   In October 2015, Allie Carter's dog shot her with a shotgun. The dog's name was Trigger.

986.   The South Pole experiences one sunset and one sunrise per year.

987.   If you crack an egg 60ft underwater, it will stay together.

988.   Caroyln Davidson designed the Nike logo in 1971. She was paid $35 for her services.

989.   The stringy part of a banana is called a phloem. It spreads nutrients around the banana to help it grow.

990.   In 2011, the red-crested tree rat appeared for two hours in North Colombia before scuttling away. This rodent was thought to be extinct for 113 years. Since 2011, this tree rat hasn't been seen since.

991. The following cats – American lion, cabcoh, carcajou, catawampas, cougar, catamount, Colorado cougar, cougouar, cuguacuara, cuguacuarana, deer cat, deer tiger, eastern cougar, Florida panther, gray lion, guasura, Indian devil, king cat, leon Americano mountain screamer, leon Colorado, leon de montana, leon sabanero, leon bayo, leopardo, long tail, Mexican lion, mountain lion, mountain tiger, onca vermelha, onca parda, painter, pampas cat, panther, plain lion, puma, purple feather, quinquajou, reditigri, Silberlowe leon, silver lion, sneak cat, sucuarana, swamp devil, swamp lion, tigre rouge, tygre, Wisconsin puma, yagua-pyta, and the Yuma cougar all have one thing in common… they are all the exact same animal!

The puma has 49 colloquial names, which is more than any other animal. Its zoological name is the pumas concolor.

992.5% of Swedish people claim to have a hypersensitivity to electromagnetism. It is the only country that recognizes electromagnetic hypersensitivity as an official functional impairment (even though it isn't real.) People with this "condition" use metallic shielding in their homes to protect themselves from dangerous EM waves. This disorder is always self-diagnosed.

993. The first female millionaire in the US was Sara Breedlove. During the 1890s, she made her fortune by selling hair products that were designed and marketed for black women.

994. Israel hired autistic people for their elite intelligence group, Unit 9900. This group study countless satellite images. Because of their autism, these members can identify tiny details that regular people miss. Since this unit has been initiated, the members have identified criminals, weapons and even found a secret weapons cache by observing satellite pictures.

995. Some rattlesnakes are evolving to hide their rattling sounds.

996. The comic strip, Garfield, was not created to be funny. According to the creator, it was only created to make a marketable character. It seemed to work since Garfield appeared in countless comic strips, got his own animated show, and two films... even

though he's not funny.

997. In 2008, a Japanese man noticed that some of his food was missing or had been moved. He decided to set up cameras around his house, assuming that someone broke in. The tapes on the camera revealed that a homeless woman had been living in his wardrobe for over a year and had been stealing his food anytime he left the house.

998. In most Western countries, the buttons on men's and women's shirts are on the opposite sides.

999. In 1561, many citizens in Nuremberg, Germany, witnessed two colossal black cylinders in the sky. These cylinders launched dozens of black and blue spheres, red crosses, and white discs. The witnesses said the objects looked like they were fighting each other. An hour later, the objects disappeared. The newspaper described it as "a very frightful spectacle." But it doesn't stop there. Five years later, a similar incident occurred in Switzerland. On August 7th 1566, the inhabitants of Basel were mystified when they saw hundreds of black spheres in the sky whirling around for

several hours. According to the town's journalist, Samuel Coccius, the spheres looked "as if they were fighting a battle, a great number of them became red and igneous, thereafter they were consumed and died out."

There has never been a plausible theory to explain what caused these incidents.

1000.   Although Usain Bolt is the fastest person in the world, he has never run a mile in one go in his entire life.

26204246R00096

Printed in Great Britain
by Amazon